ADVANCE PRAISE
for *WHY IS YOUR NAME UPSIDE DOWN?*

"Somewhere in between the all-nighters, the politics, the deadlines, the bullshit, and the insanity, the ad business manages to be fun, sometimes even joyful. David Oakley's book captures what it's like inside the hurricane. Oh, plus it's funny."

Luke Sullivan,
Author of Hey, Whipple, Squeeze This

"David Oakley has the brains to dream up crazy ideas and the guts to follow through. 'Be memorable,' he says, and this book qualifies. The moment you read these stories, you'll want to go tell your friends."

Tommy Tomlinson,
Magazine writer and former Charlotte Observer *columnist*

"At his core, David Oakley is a storyteller and a damn good one. He's been doing it for his clients and his agency for decades. Now he's done it for us. Sit down and let David take you to Oakley World."

Peter Coughter,
Professor VCU Brandcenter, President, Coughter & Company

"Target audience: You. Product benefit: Laughter. Weeping. Weeping with laughter. Subliminal message: You will buy multiple copies of this book."

Jim Mountjoy,
Director of EYE creative lab

"David Oakley isn't an advertising writer, he is a writer we are fortunate to have in advertising. For a guy who has spent a lot of his life as trickster, hustler, and self-confessed white liar, this book is incredibly open, honest, and revealing."

Susan Credle,
Chief Creative Officer, Leo Burnett USA

"In this book are ridiculously entertaining tales of the adventures of running your own advertising agency, all told by one of the best copywriters and creative directors in the business today."

David Baldwin,
Lead Guitar, Baldwin &

WHY IS YOUR NAME UPSIDE DOWN?
Stories from a Life in Advertising

DAVID OAKLEY

Donna — I'm so happy we reconnected after all these years. It makes writing the book totally worthwhile!

CARMEL SAYBROOK PUBLISHING

And you're still gorgeous!

This book is an original production of Carmel Saybrook Publishing
Carmel Saybrook Publishing
1445 S. Mint Street
Charlotte, NC 28203

Cover design by Kara Noble and Eric Roch von Rochsburg

Text design by Diana Wade

ISBN: 978-0-9909865-1-5

For Vernette...Love Vern

CONTENTS

Foreword   ix

Introduction   xiii

PART ƎNO   BooneOakley At The Beginning   1

Bush v. Gore   3

The Middle Part   23

How We Landed the Big Fish   35

Unfortunately…   39

The Curse of Celine Dion   43

There's Always FOX   51

Ping-Pong   59

Need a Great Ad? Just Lie, a Little…   67

Crying on Command   73

PART OWꓕ   How Did I Get Here?   77

Camels Under the Tree   79

A Nasty Habit   83

Cold Beer   87

The Weather Picture   91

The Hustler   99

Grasshopper Casserole   105

Out of Order   111

T-Shirt Envy   115

Pathetic Stick Figures   127

Hershey Rapper   135

Want to Be a Copywriter? Learn to Spell   141

PART THREE To The Big Apple And Back 145

Can I See Your Book? 147

Meeting the Founders of Young & Rubicam 153

Your Eyes Never Age 161

Are You Serious? 165

Sneezing on Sydney 175

Gravel in the Driveway 177

Taking Credit 185

Why Is Your Name Upside Down? 189

Tea Ya Later 191

What a Difference a Logo Makes 199

Winning 100 Grand 201

Knockout 205

Visa Las Vegas 213

PART FOUR Constant Craving 219

The Best Six-Character Tweet Ever 221

Giving It Away 227

If the Colonel Had Our Recipe, He'd Be a General 233

Hit the Biscuit 245

It's Bo Time! 257

Afterword 263

Acknowledgments 265

FOREWORD

DAVID OAKLEY IS ONE OF THE MOST ORIGINAL PEOPLE I HAVE EVER MET. And I mean "original" in the way it sounds. In a world of cookie-cutter corporate types, business types, creative types—David is David. There's no one quite like him.

Now, the word "original" is usually reserved for the artistic tyrant simmering in his own delusional importance. David is the opposite. He is a *pleasant* original. A solid member of a group that includes such talented but likable folks as Ellen Degeneres and Jimmy Fallon.

David Oakley is a very nice person in a line of work that has a lot of egomaniacs. He's a kind, considerate person, which is unusual in a field so populated by Machiavellians and narcissists. He's a person whose sense of humor actually results in very funny stories. So his book is full of the truly amusing adventures of a likable advertising leader. And that is a most unusual thing.

David has earned a tremendously successful career in advertising. I think his stories about the advertising business are on par with Jerry Della Femina's *From Those Wonderful Folks Who Gave You Pearl Harbor: Front-Line Dispatches from the Advertising Wars*. This is one of the classic advertising books of the last fifty years.

After reading David's book, you will really understand the advertising business in a way only a top practitioner can communicate. And David's credentials are superb. He counts Young & Rubicam, TBWA, Chiat/Day, and The Martin Agency among his experiences. He has also won just about every top creative award in the advertising business.

If you want to learn the ad business, this is a great book to read.

You'll get a bonus with some crazy stories that go well beyond professional advice. You'll learn how to make peace with the Celine Dion curse, how to get called "pond scum" by a political manager, and how to deal with perhaps the worst client in history.

You'll also enjoy David's obsession with certain pieces of clothing, marvel at his love of Las Vegas during March Madness, and find out how a strip club and a Catholic elementary school have something in common. His stories not only contain wonderful insights into the ad business, they also are enjoyable to just curl up in a corner and read.

As the "crusty guy in his early thirties" when I first met David as his ad professor, I am delighted to assign you this brilliant collection of stories.

—John Sweeney
Distinguished Professor
Head of the Advertising Sequence, School of Media and Journalism
University of North Carolina at Chapel Hill

INTRODUCTION

CONGRATULATIONS ON PURCHASING THIS FINE PIECE OF AMERICAN LITERATURE.

Unless, of course, you didn't buy my book and a friend just shared it with you. Normally this would make me happy, since I'm in the business of advertising and my job is telling stories that people want to share. But now I'm also in the business of selling books. I want everyone to buy their own copy so I can make a shitload of money.

However you got your hands on this book, I'm happy you're reading it. (Unless you shoplifted it. Stealing is not the way to get ahead. See "Meeting the Founders of Y&R." I learned that lesson the hard way.)

My life has been spent consciously and unconsciously advertising. From marketing *Playboy* magazines that I pilfered from the Butner Kwik Pik at the age of fourteen to losing an eleventh-grade student council election to a kid who had a clever ad campaign, I discovered the importance of advertising at an early age. I just didn't realize it was actually a profession until I was about to graduate from the University of North Carolina at Chapel Hill. But with good luck and determination, I ended up working at some of the best advertising agencies in the world, learning a ton, and then getting frustrated at how the bureaucracy weighed down my creative instincts, not to mention my mischievousness. So I decided to take my talents to South Beach. Well, South Mint Street in Charlotte, North Carolina. That's how we came to found BooneOakley.

The idea for this book came to me as I was driving home from

Chapel Hill after speaking to a class at the UNC School of Journalism. I love talking to students, and I realized that day that I had a lot to say about what it means to be different—to stand out, grab attention, and be memorable. The advertising business is really a storytelling business. Brand stories. People stories. Relationship stories. Sad stories. Happy stories. Funny stories. Dumb stories. This book is my way of sharing some of the lessons my stories have taught me.

In these pages, I talk about how some of our best (and worst) ideas came to light. I talk about my superstitions, my obsessions (like writing this book), my fears, and my anxieties. I talk about being a husband, a dad, and about just being a guy. I share stories about a few of the biggest jerks I've ever met—and about some of the best people you'd ever want to meet.

I've been making ads for nearly three decades now. You know, I've heard it said that *"time slips away and leaves you with nothing, Mister, but boring stories of glory days."* Damn it! I'm living a Bruce Springsteen song, and it's not "Thunder Road."

Despite all the cool things going on in new media and digital these days, I remain a traditionalist. I still love big highway billboards. Outdoor advertising is one of my favorite media, and over the course of my career I've created a lot of fine ads on billboards.

Now here's the irony. To be effective, a billboard ad is usually eight words or less. So how is it that a guy who makes his living writing eight-word billboards has just sold you a 70,000-word book? That's almost 8,750 eight-word billboards. That's a *lot* of billboards. Actually, it's about the same number of advertising messages that you see each and every day. Isn't that a crazy number? But you know what's even crazier? Trying to make your ad stand out amid all the verbal, written, and visual noise that bombards us constantly. But that's what I try to do, every day.

I submitted a manuscript of this book to some publishers and got some serious interest. But they all wanted me to make it into a marketing textbook, like *Ten Steps to Doing Breakthrough Advertising* or something. I decided I didn't want this book to be that. I wanted to be able to write an entire chapter on dogs doing it. I wanted to write about my death wish for one of the most famous singers in the world. So once again, I'm going out on my own, just as I did when I cofounded my own ad agency nearly fifteen years ago. Like Sinatra said, "I did it my way."

I hope that you find *Why Is Your Name Upside Down?* as much fun to read as it has been for me to write. I've tried to write the stories the way I'd tell them if I was sitting across the table from you at Olde Mecklenburg Brewery, sipping on a Captain Jack Pilsner.[*]

About the title: It's a question that I've been asked at least a thousand times since we opened BooneOakley. Everyone wants to know why Oakley is upside down. Inside you'll find out why. I will tell you this now: our logo certainly gets noticed. At least once a week, someone comes to the front door of the agency to tell us that our sign is upside down. Seriously. You can't make that stuff up.

Now that my book is done, I feel a great sense of accomplishment. Not only because I finally finished it, but because you bought it. I knew you would. I've been getting people to buy things that they didn't want or need for twenty-seven years.

---

[*] The folks at Olde Mecklenburg Brewery promised me free beer for a year if I mentioned them in a story. This widely-used form of advertising is called *product placement*.

PART ƎNO
BOONEOAKLEY AT THE BEGINNING

WELCOME TO THE BOOK. You're in for a huge treat.[*]
It's OK to make mistakes.[**] We started our agency with one. You're about to read about it: the Bush-Gore billboard that we put up on BooneOakley's first day of business has influenced everything that we have done since. That kind of fearlessness became part of our DNA. It allowed us to sell breakthrough creative work that most agencies would find much too risky to present. To us, the bigger risk is being boring. And that's a risk we aren't willing to take.

---

[*]My publicist made me say that.

[**]I'm not saying that you made a mistake by buying this book. But if after reading it, if you think you wasted your money, I will refund your $20 if you will meet me in Vegas during March Madness.

BUSH V. GORE

TWO WEEKS BEFORE THE 2000 PRESIDENTIAL ELECTION, JOHN BOONE AND I LEFT OUR CUSHY JOBS AS CREATIVE DIRECTORS AT THE MARTIN AGENCY TO START OUR OWN AD AGENCY. It was the fulfillment of a lifelong dream. It was a big moment. But it wasn't anywhere near as big as our first ad. On the same day we started BooneOakley, we posted a highway billboard with a photo of George Bush and the caption *Gore 2000*. Within hours, it became an international sensation.

The billboard idea came about one morning at the office when Boone and I were talking about how annoying it was that everyone puts election signs in their yards. I told him, "The last thing that I want to see when I back out of my driveway and start my drive to the office is Pat McCrory's smiling face on a sign saying 'Vote for me for mayor.' I have nothing against Pat. I've met him and he's a nice guy. I just don't want to see ten pictures of him before I get to Carmel Road. This morning, I counted twenty-seven election signs on Crooked Oak Lane alone."

"It's the same in my neighborhood," Boone said. "Last Saturday morning, a guy put a big 4-foot-by-5-foot Bush for President sign in his yard across the street from me. By Saturday evening, the houses on either side had big Al Gore signs. It's almost as competitive as Christmas lights."

"Could you imagine what would happen if someone printed an election sign wrong? Like if they put Al Gore's face on a Bush for

President ad?"

"Now *that* would get a lot of attention," Boone said.

"The media loves mistakes," I said to Boone. "You know about Yonkers Raceway in New York?"

"No," he replied.

"Apparently when that track was completed in the early 1900s, the builders were broke and didn't have any money to advertise the track. So the day before the first race, they installed ten-foot-tall letters on the entrance facing the highway that spelled YONKERS RACEWYA. The mistake got them front-page coverage in the *New York Times* and the *New York Post*. Thanks to all the press, the race sold out and they were never broke again. They misspelled it on purpose. Or at least that's what they said."

"That's wild. I never heard that before," Boone said with what I perceived as total disinterest. He was used to hearing my encyclopedic knowledge of useless information. He went back to his office to play his favorite video game, Unreal Tournament.

About an hour later, Boone came back over to my desk. "We should find a client for that."

"For what?"

"That Gore-Bush yard sign idea."

"What kind of client could use a crazy idea like that?" I asked.

"One thing's for sure—whoever printed the yard signs would be out of a job, so maybe we should do it for a job-finder client like Monster.com," Boone suggested.

I suddenly remembered a job-listings agency in Charlotte. "There's 123hire.com here. I just saw one of their billboards."

"Let's call 'em."

Three days later, the president of 123hire.com, Brian Parsley, was in our office. We explained the idea and told him that we thought it would get a lot of attention for his company. The only problem was that the election was less than a month away, and he'd have to commit to buy billboard space that day. We knew that this could be a major sticking point, because it would seem like we were just trying to sell the guy ad space. But Brian was a smart guy. And after he saw the idea, he knew that we weren't selling ad space.

Boone broke the silence and asked, "So what do you think?"

Brian rubbed his chin and said, "I'm a risk taker. And I like this idea. I like it a lot. But I don't like to take risks with my money. But the way I see this idea, there's no risk. You know why there's no risk?"

"Because it's a really good idea?" I asked nervously.

"Well, yes, David, it is a good idea. But the real reason there's no risk is that I *have* a billboard on Interstate 485 near Pineville that needs new creative."

"What?" Boone and I responded in unison.

"This will be perfect for that location. When can you have it installed?"

"It'll take a couple of weeks to print it," Boone said.

"Great. Let's do it."

We shook hands and the deal was done. At our first BooneOakley client meeting, we'd sold our first campaign, two weeks before our official start date. We were ahead of the game.

Now we had to figure out a way to make our idea happen. We couldn't exactly schedule a photo shoot with George Bush, so we decided to look into buying a stock image. We had no idea how much that might cost and we were shocked at the price: a mere $150 to use (then) Governor Bush's image on an outdoor board.

Our motto had always been, "It's easier to ask for forgiveness than it is to get permission," but we decided buying the image would be a wise investment. That way, if the Bush campaign chose to sue us, we could truthfully say that we had permission to use it. We also decided to alter the *Gore 2000* typeface just enough that we technically weren't using his actual logo. The last thing we wanted was to get sued. But we figured both campaigns had better things to do than come after a start-up agency in North Carolina whose most valuable assets were a Kiss pinball machine and a Piggly Wiggly sign.

But then a more daunting question arose: *How in the hell are we going to keep this scheme quiet?* It's not like we were going to print the ad out at Kinko's and run out and stick it in someone's yard in the middle of the night. We needed help. We needed accomplices. Accomplices who could keep their mouths shut.

But I knew people. Shady people. Secretive people. Like Gale Bonnell, Barry Asman, and Mark Bartlett at Adams Outdoor, a billboard company. They could do it. Especially Gale. She'd love the idea. She loved any idea that would promote the power of outdoor advertising. And there was no denying that this one did that.

Gale and Barry agreed to go along with our plan. On Friday, October 20, we'd post the billboard with Bush's face and Gore's logo. We'd leave it up over the weekend and we would "fix" it the following Monday with an overlay (banner) announcing a job opening for a proofreader on 123hire.com. If anyone called Adams about the "mistake," they'd say they were aware of it and would take care of it ASAP. Now we had to show it to Mark Bartlett, Adams' operations manager. He was their "make-it-happen" guy. Mark took one look at the board and said in his Mint Hill drawl, "Y'all are crazy. Just plain crazy."

"Well, do you like it?"

"I don't like it. I *love* it. This is the kind of stuff that makes my job fun. I'm living the dream. And next weekend, we're going to be living the scheme."

Mark and his crew don't work in the rain. If it had continued raining like it had done all that week, the board might not have been installed until after the election. But on the morning of October 20, there wasn't a cloud in the sky. When Boone pulled his Isuzu to the shoulder of I-485, we saw an incredible sight. Our billboard was already up. And the crew was climbing down.

We got out of the car and walked over to the fence near the billboard. Mark met us on the other side of the fence. He was grinning from ear to ear. "When we got out here and unwrapped the vinyl, one of my men told me there was a mistake on the board. I told him, 'Put it up anyway. The ad agency approved it.' Then another one said, 'We'll just have to take it down, Mark.' And I said, 'That's right. And they'll have to pay us extra to do it. So shut up and put the board up.' So they put it up." Mark looked over his shoulder at the billboard, laughed out loud, shook his head, and said, "Y'all ain't right. Y'all are just plain crazy."

October 20, 2000: the biggest blunder in presidential campaign history goes up on Interstate 485 in Charlotte.

The three of us stood on the side of I-485 and watched motorists driving by at 75 mph. No one was even so much as glancing at the board.

"But no one's looking at it," I said in frustration.

Mark laughed and said, "If these jackalopes noticed it"—pointing to his crew—"those jackolopes will notice it." Then he pointed to the cars whizzing by. "Give 'em time, David."

We had a plan if anyone actually noticed the board. We figured that they would call Adams Outdoor to point out the mistake. So we wrote a script for the receptionist at Adams to follow. Her task was simple: thank the person for calling and say that Adams was aware of the board and that she would have an account executive call them back. Pretty foolproof. Or so we thought.

On our way back to the office, we decided to grab some lunch. We chowed down on burritos and had a few laughs about what a crazy week it had been. But more than anything, we were just waiting. Waiting for someone to notice the board. *Jesus, it had been up for an hour and forty-five minutes. And it hadn't even got a single reaction.* Bush and Gore were just sitting out there all by themselves on 485 and no one gave a shit. What a freakin' letdown. Then my cell phone rang.

It was Barry Asman, the general manager from Adams Outdoor.

"David, it's Barry from Adams."

"How's it going, Barry?"

"Not so good."

"What do you mean?"

"We just got a call from a reporter at FOX News about the billboard."

"Awesome. What'd you say?"

"I didn't say anything. He left a message."

"Well, call him back."

I could tell by the tone of Barry's voice that something wasn't quite right. He wasn't his normal jovial self. "David, when we agreed to be a part of this prank, we agreed to field calls from motorists who had noticed the mistake. We hadn't bargained on talking with the press."

"C'mon Barry, we talked about the possibility that some of the local TV would cover it."

"This isn't local, David, this is FOX News National," he said.

"Ohhhhh," I said through a smile I'm sure he could see over the phone.

"Adams is a large company, David. We just can't have it coming out in the press that we made this kind of mistake."

At that moment, I saw everything crashing down. All of our efforts, all of our planning, all of our everything, all for naught. This was going to be a total flop. Everything was going to fall apart. I panicked for a second, then took a deep breath and calmly said, "Well, we're not a large company. So give anyone who calls my cell number."

"What should I tell the reporter?"

"Tell the reporter that the agency printed the vinyl and it was shipped directly to Adams. Make it clear that Adams Outdoor did not print the board. Tell them if they want to get to the bottom of it, they'll have to talk with the ad agency that created the board." I could feel Barry's relief through the phone.

"Thanks."

"Have that reporter call me."

I told Boone that a FOX News reporter had just called Adams and that he was going to call us in a few minutes.

The look on his face was priceless. It was that unmistakable look that you get when you reach the top of the first hill of a rollercoaster. That anticipation-dread-excitement-fear combo that happens right before all hell breaks loose. It was easy to recognize, because I felt it spreading over my own face at the same time.

"Do you want to talk with the reporter?" I asked Boone.

"No, you're better at this sort of thing."

"What do you mean 'this sort of thing'?"

"Lying."

"Lying?" I asked incredulously.

"I just don't feel comfortable saying that the billboard was a mistake. Because it really isn't a mistake."

"OK, I'll talk with the reporter."

Not five seconds later, my phone rang.

"BooneOakley," I answered for the first time with our new agency's name.

"Hi, this is Brian Kelly from FOX News. May I speak with David Oakley?"

"Yes, I'll put you through to his office."

I waited ten seconds.

"Hello, this is David."

"Hi, this is Brian Kelly from FOX News in New York. Are you the ones responsible for the campaign billboard in Charlotte?"

"Which one?" I asked coyly.

"The one that shows Governor Bush's picture and says 'Gore 2000.'"

"Yes, I'm aware of the...um...mix-up." I raised my eyebrows to Boone.

I was careful not to call the board a mistake. I knew I shouldn't outright lie to the reporters. But I could certainly bend the truth. The billboard was not a mistake. It was completely intentional. It was a mix-up. A billboard specifically designed to mix up reporters.

"How could this happen?" Brian asked.

"Honestly this is our first week in business, we're a new ad agency, and I guess it was an oversight in our production department."

"So what campaign are you working for? The Republicans or the Democrats?"

I thought for a second and said, "Well...we've been instructed not to say."

"By who?"

"We've...we've been instructed not to say," I said.

Brian didn't particularly like this answer. I guess he was used to politicians being evasive.

"I can find out very easily who hired you. You might as well just tell me."

"You gotta understand, clearly our client is upset about this and I'm just saying what they asked me to say."

"I'll bet they are upset. When will you have the mistake fixed?"

"We would like to do it immediately, but it's Friday afternoon and all of the outdoor crews have left for the weekend. We hope to get the mix-up fixed on Monday."

"Could you give me the correct spelling of your name and your company?"

"D-A-V-I-D O-A-K-L-E-Y. B-O-O-N-E-O-A-K-L-E-Y, no space."

It was at this point that I knew they were going to run a story, so I couldn't resist amping up my southern accent and asking, "You're not really going to put this little billboard on the news, are you?"

"Are you kidding? This is the biggest screw-up of the presidential campaign."

"Ohhhhh noooo," I groaned falsely.

"Thank you for your time, Mr. Oakley."

Over the next two hours, this call was repeated at least a dozen times. CNN, ABC News, United Press International, CBS News, CBS Radio, NBC *Nightly News* and even the *Washington Post* called. My only disappointment was that we didn't get a call from the *Weekly World News*. I guess they know a hoax when they see one.

The best call of the afternoon wasn't from a reporter. It was from Ned Grant, the Vice Chairman of the Republican Party.

"BooneOakley," I answered.

"David, I'll bet that I'm not the first person who's called you today about the billboard," he said lightheartedly.

"You are right, Mr. Grant."

"Well, the reason I'm calling is that your billboard has my candidate's picture on it."

"Yes, um, it does." I said, thanking God that we paid the $150 to the stock photo house for permission to use the photo of Bush.

"We need you to take it down."

"We're working on it. But the billboard installation crew has gone for the weekend."

"This is the type of mistake that can swing an election," he giddily replied, "and I must say, I'm really happy that you're not working for the GOP."

"I don't know if we're going to be working for anyone after this," I responded, dejected.

"Well, I don't know if you will either," he chuckled. "Just get it down as soon as you can. We don't like having Governor Bush's face next to that four-letter word."

"Four-letter word?" I asked.

"G-O-R-E. That's four letters," he said and howled with laughter. "Just get it down as soon as you can."

It was all I could do not to remind him that Bush was a four-letter word as well, and in certain circles, it was much more offensive. But I bit my tongue.

"We will, Mr. Grant. We'll get it changed by Monday."

"Good. Hope the weekend is better for you than today."

"Me too," I said, and we hung up.

As soon as the conversation ended, I knew exactly where he was coming from. Unlike most of the reporters, this guy had done some research. Ned Grant knew for a fact that BooneOakley wasn't hired to do a campaign billboard by the Republican Party or the Bush campaign. This could only mean one thing: the Democratic Party or the Gore campaign had royally screwed up. Ned Grant was reveling in the fact that this was not going to be easy for the Democrats to explain. In an election this close, this could be the thing that put the Republicans back in the White House. No wonder he was in such a good mood.

Our moods, on the other hand, were swinging like a pair of donkey balls. One minute, Boone and I were high-fiving each other that this was the most amazing stunt we had ever pulled off, and the next we were almost hyperventilating.

"Oh my God! Oh my God! This is great! This is awesome!"

"Oh my God! Oh my God! This is not good! This is going to be a disaster!"

We knew if word got out that we had intentionally screwed up the campaign billboard, the focus of the media coverage on Monday would not be on 123hire.com.

It would only be on us. And we were going to be the laughing-stocks of the ad world.

I said to Boone, "If this happens, the whole thing will be a colossal failure and a complete waste of their money."

"Wait a minute. He only paid us $3000. Has he ever gotten any press for any of his other boards?"

"I doubt it."

"OK, then. We rock."

We started high-fiving again.

Later that afternoon, I heard Boone let out a whoop.

"Check this out!"

He was pointing at his computer screen. "Look at this!" he shouted with glee. He was looking at CNN.com and the lead story was AD AGENCY BUNGLES CAMPAIGN BILLBOARD. There for the world to see was a picture of our billboard. I stood looking over his shoulder in stunned disbelief. Even though I'd talked with a dozen reporters in the last two hours, actually seeing a story on it almost left me speechless.

"Now that's really cool," I managed.

"But you know what's really, really cool?" Boone asked me.

"What?"

"Gore and Bush are going to see that billboard."

"Well, come November 7, one of them is going to need a job. Maybe he'll contact 123hire.com."

"Now that would be really, really, really cool," Boone said.

Suddenly our little stunt was starting to get kind of huge. I mean, we'd already heard from most of the national news networks and the RNC. This story was going global. I was excited. And scared shitless. On my way home, I called my wife, Claire, to give her an update and find out if she needed me to pick up anything from the store. Claire knew all about our stunt. She interrupted me.

"Karen Summers [our neighbor] just came by to see if you were OK. She said that they were talking about you on the radio and she was so sorry about what happened. I thought you were in an accident or something."

"What were they saying? What station?"

"WBT. They were saying that you and Boone are a couple of dumb-asses."

"Well, they got that right. Do you need anything from the Harris Teeter?"

"No, just get your dumb ass home." Claire giggled.

I hung up and immediately tuned to 1110 WBT talk radio. What I heard bordered on the surreal. *How often are you listening to your car radio and you hear someone talking about you?* I guess it happens to politicians and celebrities all the time, but not to advertising guys.

WBT's drive-time host was in full rant:

"...and these imbeciles at the BooneOakley agency don't even have a phone listing. If any of you in our audience this afternoon

know the idiots at BooneOakley agency, please tell them to get in touch with us. And if Boone and Oakley are listening, please call in and explain how anyone could be so stupid as to not know the difference between Al Gore and Governor Bush. That is, if you are educated enough to know how to dial a phone. Let's go to the phones. Jimmy from Gastonia, you're on the air."

"I think this billboard has just reinforced the stereotype of how dumb southerners are. Not all of us southerners are as stupid as you two, Boone and Oakley. But now the whole world thinks we are. Thanks a lot."

I drove home realizing that I needed to spend the next three days acting like an idiot. Which really wouldn't be that hard. I'd just be myself.

Early Saturday morning, I saw our billboard again on the ground at the end of our driveway. It was smack-dab on the front page of the *Charlotte Observer.* The caption read, VOTE FOR WHOM? I went back inside and googled *campaign billboard.* There were 117 stories about it online. All over the world, people were talking and writing about our blunder. My favorite was from a publication in Beijing. I'd never visited a Chinese website before, but there was our billboard, surrounded by a thousand Chinese characters. You didn't need to know the language to translate it. It said, I believe, "Stupid Americans. They don't know the difference between their presidential candidates. No wonder they say they can't tell us apart. What a bunch of douchebags."

On Sunday morning, Claire, Sydney, Lucas, and I went to church. We don't go every Sunday, but for some reason, I really felt the need to go that Sunday. I guess I needed to ask forgiveness for all of my half-truths of the last couple of days. When we got home the phone was ringing. I ran inside and picked it up. It was Boone.

"It's Sunday morning. Why aren't you in church?" I answered jokingly.

"I just got home from church."

"So did I."

"Wow, this is an unusual weekend," Boone said.

"It is," I agreed. "What's up?"

"I just wanted to tell you what happened at church. After the service, Tammy and I were waiting in line outside to tell the pastor that we enjoyed the sermon. When we got up to him, I said, 'I enjoyed the sermon.' 'Thank you,' he said. Then he looked me in the eye and said, 'I heard about the billboard, John.' Then he put his other arm on my shoulder and said, 'I'm praying for you.'"

"Are you kidding me? Did you tell him?"

"I said, 'Just stay tuned. There's more to come.' And I winked."

"You winked at your pastor?"

"Yeah."

"Did he wink back?"

"No."

"Well, you know how some pastors are."

I hung the phone up and noticed that the message light was flashing. It was a message from our friend Marcy Walsh, who is a PR executive in Los Angeles: *"This is Marcy. I'm at the gym and I'm on a treadmill watching* Headline News, *and all of a sudden a story comes on about a billboard in Charlotte and then I realized that you did it. Oh, I am so sorry that this has happened to you. This is not good. Please call me back when you get a chance, but my advice to you is you have to come out and admit that you made a horrible mistake. I know this isn't how you intended your agency to start and honestly, I'm not sure that you'll be able to survive it. But the first thing that you need to do is admit that you made a mistake. Don't avoid the press. Please call me."*

I knew I had to call her back. I had made it all the way to Sunday without letting the cat out of the bag, but Marcy was a good friend and she was genuinely concerned for us. I called her.

"Hi Marcy. You're up early."

"Oh David, are you OK?" she asked, almost frantic.

"Yes, we're fine."

"Well, I saw the story on the news about the billboard. I'm so sorry that this has happened to you guys. What you need to do is call a press conference Monday morning and tell them that it was an honest mistake that could happen to anyone.

"Marcy," I interrupted. "I appreciate your concern. But I've got to tell you something and you can't tell anyone."

"Oh God…there's more to it?"

"There is…can you keep a secret?"

"Yes."

"OK. Are you ready?"

"I guess," she said apprehensively.

"We did it on purpose."

"You what?"

"We did it on purpose. It's for our first client, 123hire.com. We're going to put a banner over the Bush picture and Gore logo tomorrow that explains the whole thing."

"Oh my God!" she screamed. "It wasn't a mistake?"

"Nope."

She was quiet for a couple of moments. I think she was just letting it all sink in. Then she said, "This is completely unbelievable. You've fooled CNN."

"And the *Atlanta Constitution* and FOX News and the *Washington Post*."

"Oh my God. This is the most amazing PR coup I've ever heard of."

This was the first true outside validation that this scheme was going to work, and it felt really good to hear it. But I still wasn't ready to announce, "Mission accomplished."

"Well, we've got to keep it quiet until tomorrow for it to be a success. Do you think that the press will cover it when we 'fix' the board?"

"They have to cover it. Right now not only is it a major fuck-up, it's a major mystery. The world wants to know who hired you. The world wants to know who fucked up!"

> As you may recall, President Bush made his own billboard-style mistake a couple years later by prematurely putting a Mission Accomplished banner on an aircraft carrier long before the Iraq war was over.

"But will the reporters cover it when they realize that *they* were the ones who fucked up?"

"Hmmm…you may have a point. You did lie to them."

"I didn't lie to them. I told them it was a mix-up."

Marcy laughed. "OK, so you duped them. Either way, they might not be so ready to give you credit for pulling it off."

"I really don't care about credit for us, that'll come later. I just want to be sure that they report that the board was for 123hire.com."

"Either way, awesome way to start your agency."

One of the most amazing things about the whole shenanigan was that none of the reporters really questioned us. I mean really, no one ever thought to really question Boone or me about the billboard. Or no one put two and two together that those wacky ad guys might be up to something. We thought that as soon as the reporters heard that an agency named BooneOakley was behind it, they would instantly know that it was some sort of a prank. I guess that just goes to show you how large our egos were. We actually thought everyone knew us. The truth is that no one knows ad people except other ad people. And the other seven billion people on the planet don't want to know us.

On Monday morning, Boone and I met at our office at 7:45 a.m. Boone was there first and was watching *Good Morning America* when I walked in. We were meeting early because Adams was scheduled to fix the billboard that morning and we wanted to make sure the news coverage continued. We decided we should write a press release to announce when the billboard would be fixed. Then something on the TV caught our ear. We turned and saw Antonio Mora, *Good Morning America*'s news anchor, sharing the screen with the Bush/Gore billboard. Antonio smiled as he read the teleprompter:

> *Even though the candidates are neck and neck, not even the tightest poll numbers find them this close. The advertising people who designed this billboard in Charlotte, North Carolina, say their mix-up will be fixed by this week. And then we will know which candidate's billboard it really is supposed to be. That's the news at 8:05, time now for the weather, and Tony Perkins, a big mistake there...*

They cut outside to Tony Perkins on a New York street with tons of tourists behind him and he says, "I wonder what the guys who designed that billboard are doing now for a living?" Then they all busted up laughing.

The guys who designed that billboard were cobbling together a press release. Fifteen minutes later, we were faxing it to the local NBC, ABC, and CBS affiliates. It stated simply, "The campaign bilboard on I-485 in Charlotte will be changed on Monday at 11:00 a.m." Yes, we misspelled *billboard*. No, we didn't do it on purpose. Without a doubt, it was one of the most poorly crafted press releases in press release history, but it was effective.

At eleven a.m., an NBC News helicopter hovered above our billboard, filming live as the Adams Outdoor crew posted a yellow banner across the board that read:

Today's job opening: Proofreader. 123hire.com.

October 23, 2000: the "mix-up" was fixed.

One hour later, the footage was on *Headline News* with this pithy report:

> *When it comes to politics, take nothing at face value. When this billboard first went up in Charlotte, North Carolina, everyone considered it a blunder. After all, it shows Governor Bush's face and Al Gore's name. But today it was revealed that this was a publicity stunt for 123hire.com. The ad agency executive says he is pleased with the nationwide coverage. I'll bet they are, huh? But Gore's people are not laughing. They say the billboard wrongfully confused people in North Carolina.*

Not long after, my phone started ringing again. First it was CBS Radio. Then it was the Associated Press. Then came the *Wall Street Journal*. They called us all kinds of names. *Genius. Brilliant. Inno-*

vative. Bold. Daring. And just plain *funny*. It was unbelievable. Even though the joke was on them, they all took it very well. Well, almost everyone.

"David Oakley?" said the voice on the other end of the line. "This is Ned Grant, Vice Chairman of the Republican Party."

"Hi, Ned. Nice to hear from you again."

"Mr. Oakley, you are pond scum. You are vermin. You are lower than low."

"Well. I'm sorry you feel that way, Mr. Grant."

"A scuz bucket, that's what you are Oakley. The way you used my candidate's photo on that billboard is a disgrace. You deceived voters."

"Your candidate's photo? He's my candidate, too."

"You're a Republican?" Suddenly Ned was as friendly as Doris Day.

"The entire Oakley family is Republican. We're 279 strong in eastern North Carolina."

"Really now? Well, I didn't know you were one of us."

"I was until a minute ago. But I don't vote for anybody who calls me pond scum. Now I'll make sure no one else in my family votes for Governor Bush either. Thanks for the call. You just swung North Carolina to the Democrats."

And I hung up on him.

Boone, who'd been listening to the entire conversation, looked at me and said, "You're not a Republican."

"And that wasn't a reporter. So I lied to him."

And BooneOakley was up and running.

THE MIDDLE PART

"STEP AWAY FROM THE LEDGE," A VOICE INSTRUCTED.
I was right in the middle of presenting a storyboard to the marketing team at Turner Network Television when we heard the commotion outside. I paused for a second, and then continued explaining how this new campaign would be perfect for TNT.

Then we heard it again: "Step away from the ledge." It was coming from a bullhorn.

"What the hell is that?" Greg Johns, TNT's marketing director, blurted out, interrupting me.

He stood up and walked over to the window. He opened the shades to get a view of what was happening below. "Oh my God!" he exclaimed. We all scurried over to see what was going on.

"Please step away from the ledge, now," the voice instructed again. "Do not jump." We looked down from our fourth floor window, and saw five or six Atlanta firemen looking up at the building. We then heard a voice yell down at them from above our floor. A couple more firemen ran up, carrying a rescue net.

At the same time we all realized: *there is someone on the top of the TNT building who's about to jump.*

"Please back away from the ledge," the fireman with the bullhorn pleaded again as the other firemen got the rescue net in place.

The eight people in the conference room were now gape-mouthed, our noses pressed against the tinted glass windows, watching the tragedy about to unfold. I'd like to think that the ad campaign I was presenting was interesting, but it didn't have nearly the attraction of a distraught person contemplating taking her own life.

"Ma'am, please sit down. Sit down," the fireman implored.

A moment later a body flashed by our window. It passed in a split second blur—a person, flailing helplessly against the pull of gravity.

"Noooooo," screamed one of the people in the room. The rest of us let out a startled gasp in unison.

We looked down to see the woman's body strike the safety net with so much force that it bounced wildly to the side, careening completely off the net and landing with a thud on the asphalt parking lot. The woman's wig flew off her head and settled in a clump beside the front tire of a BMW, just feet from her limp body. Was she dead? Had she survived?

Jennifer Dorian from TNT shrieked and grabbed my arm in horror.

The firemen made no effort to assist the woman. Instead they flipped their safety net over to reveal a TNT logo on the other side. Beneath the logo was message—a message that was directed at the eight people in our conference room.

It said: *TNT. We Know Drama.*

Three weeks of careful planning had gone into this stunt. It was designed to get the marketing team at TNT to remember us—a small upstart agency named BooneOakley. We had to do something unforgettable since we were pitching against Mother and Goodby Silverstein, two of the best and most well-known creative agencies in the world.

We had demonstrated to the cable channel that we knew drama, maybe even better than they did. And that we were the ad agency that could come up with dramatic ways to show the world that TNT was television's destination for drama.

Our presentation went off exactly as planned.

Twenty-one days earlier, the BooneOakley team[*] had gathered in our conference room, as our account executive, Jessica Stanfield, went through the brief.

"Here is the single most compelling idea for this assignment: TNT wants to be known as the destination station for drama programming. It's the place to go to watch *L.A. Law, Hill Street Blues,* and *Barnaby Jones.*"

"There's no drama on TNT. All they show are reruns of *Andy Griffith* and the Atlanta Braves," one of our art directors piped in, clearly thinking that creative briefs were a ridiculous waste of time.[**]

"You're thinking of TBS, TNT's sister station. In the last couple of years, TNT has been changing to dramatic programming," Jessica explained.

Sometimes, it seems that it's the creative team's job to dispute everything an account person says. Sure, they were excited about the prospect of working on TNT's business, but they knew that coming up with a big creative idea is not an easy thing to do. It's infinitely more difficult than writing a creative brief.

From the creative team's perspective, once the brief is written, the account person's work is done. (Unless you consider kissing the client's ass "work.") More often than not, copywriters and art directors take issue with the brief for one simple reason: They're upset that now it's their turn to work.

Then I heard the question that I hear every single time I'm in a

---

[*]*A creative team at BooneOakley usually consists of a copywriter, an art director, a designer, a digital strategist, an account executive, an account planner, and a media specialist.*

[**]*A creative brief is a document created through initial meetings, interviews, readings, and discussions between a client and agency before any work begins. It's designed to inform and guide the work throughout the assignment.*

briefing session. It came from Adam Roth, our art director: "How in the world are we going to do anything good based on this brief?"

"Look, guys," I said, "I read somewhere that a brief is a good brief if you can see a truth in it. As hard to believe as it might be, the truth is that TNT is changing their programming to be more dramatic. They want to stand for something. They have chosen to stand for drama. So no matter how loudly your gut is screaming that this brief was bullshit, it is, in fact, truthful. TNT is in the process of a major makeover. Our job is to figure out how to convince the world that TNT is no longer a hodgepodge of nonrelated programming you occasionally stumble upon while channel-surfing. They want people to intentionally choose their station. If you want to watch dramatic programming, there's one place to go. Our job is to make TNT the destination for drama."

Wow, I had just convinced the room that the brief was spot on. Not an easy task, if I do say so myself.

I used to wish I was married to Samantha Stephens, the girl from *Bewitched*. I had a huge crush on her when I was a kid, but as I grew older what I really found attractive about Sam was her magic. She could just wiggle her nose and suddenly her husband, ad man Darrin Stephens, would have a killer new campaign to present to his client.

How awesome would that be? One wiggle of Sam's nose and she completely cuts out the part between the brief and the presentation. The Middle Part. Not the middle part that we used to wear in our hair in the '80s to achieve those luxurious, balanced, feathered bangs like Farrah had. The Middle Part that I'm talking about is simply hard work.

The Middle Part is when you wake up at three a.m. with an idea that you think is fantastic, go back to sleep with a smile on your face, and then can't remember it in the morning. Or you get up to write it down, convinced that it's the greatest idea ever, and when you wake up in the morning you read what you wrote and your idea is a Linda Lovelace: it sucks.

The Middle Part is exasperating. The Middle Part is confusing. The Middle Part is unpredictable. The Middle Part is a series of dead ends. It's also an exercise in figuring out how to get around dead ends. It's problem solving. It's invigorating and it's insanely nutty. The Middle Part is that no-man's-land between the brief and the presentation. Without a doubt, the Middle Part is the most frustrating part of this business. But sometimes, it's also the most fun.

As soon as the TNT briefing was done, we entered the Middle Part. We worked night and day for a couple of weeks and came up with three different integrated campaigns that we believed would cause disruption in the marketplace. Three ideas that would cause people to stop what they were doing and take notice. But we knew ideas alone wouldn't be enough. To win, we needed to do something dramatic. We needed to cause a disruption in our meeting.

We needed some drama. Faking a heart attack mid-meeting was suggested, as was threatening to jump out the window if they didn't buy our campaign.

I told the team how when I was at Young & Rubicam a guy jumped from the fourteenth floor. An art director who worked there said he looked up from his computer as a body flashed by his window. He opened his window, looked down and saw the man's body on the awning of a bagel shop. That awning was never the same.

"That's it! That's it!" Boone shouted. "We'll have someone jump off the roof of the TNT building. And we'll watch it fall by."

"Who are we going to get to jump off the building?" I had a few people I wanted to nominate.

"Adam!"

I looked at Adam, who I viewed as a valuable asset. "We're not going to throw Adam off the building."

"No, but he could throw a dummy off. And it would look like a real person trying to kill themselves."

That's how crazy advertising ideas are hatched. One guy says something and it spurs an idea from the next person.

This was a killer idea. Vile, but killer. That's how true magic happens. Sam could wiggle her nose, but we could "throw" Adam off a four-story building just to win an account. This idea wasn't just a brainstorm—it was a brain-hurricane.

Then the eye passed over. Everything got real quiet. We could hear the birds outside again. This idea was nuts. How would it work?

When the dummy hit the ground, we worried the TNT executives would know it was fake. Or what if someone in the room had lost a family member or friend to suicide?

Someone came to the rescue. "The dummy doesn't have to die. We could have some brave person save the dummy!"

"Save the dummy?"

"Yeah. Like maybe some Atlanta firemen or someone like that."

We couldn't ask real firemen to take a break from saving real lives to save our dummy just so we could win an account. How selfish!

Someone then suggested we contact some students at Creative Circus, an advertising school in Atlanta, and ask them to stand in as actors. Advertising students will do just about anything for their portfolios. We'd dress them up as firemen. But we needed some real fireman suits, not those shitty ones they sell at costume shops for Halloween. And, we'd need to jerry-rig a net that the "firemen" would use to "save" our dummy.

The next morning on the way to work, I passed the fire station on South Boulevard. I thought, *What the hell, I'll try to borrow them*, and I turned my Accord around and parked in front of the station.

A handsome fireman greeted me. "Hi, I'm Captain Jeff Alphin. Can I help you?"

"I know this might sound strange, but I'd like to borrow a few fireman suits."

"What do you need them for?" he asked.

"I'm a part of an ad agency in town. We're doing a presentation at TNT in Atlanta and we are going to throw a dummy off the top of the building and we are going to hire students to catch the dummy in a safety net. And we need fireman suits for the students to wear. It's a promotion for TNT." I realized as I was telling him all this it sounded like I was either totally full of shit or just plain out of my mind. Maybe both.

Captain Alphin eyed me for a moment, and then to my surprise kind of chuckled and said, "Well, OK."

"So can I borrow a few?"

"No, these coats are government issue. We can't just let you borrow them. But I do have some in the basement. They've been used a lot and have burn marks on them and the protective insulation is worn out. We were going to throw them away."

In the basement I saw a stack of old fireman coats and helmets. I couldn't believe my good fortune. He handed me a couple of big black garbage bags and we stuffed the coats and helmets inside. I thanked him profusely, but I couldn't help asking for one more thing. "Do you have a safety net?"

"Sorry, can't help you with that one." I thanked him again and carried the bags to the car.

I returned to the agency carrying two sacks over my back. "Ho, ho, ho, Merry Christmas."

Boone was beaming and standing by a trampoline top leaning against the wall with a three-foot-wide TNT logo with *We Know Drama* printed on it.

"Feast your eyes on our safety net."

"Oh my God, that's perfect. Where'd you get it?"

"It was in my backyard. The girls don't play on it any more so I took it apart and brought it in. What's in the bags?"

I was so excited about the trampoline that I forgot that I had the fireman suits. I opened the bags and put on a fire coat and a helmet.

"We just might win this pitch."

We had everything we needed, except for one thing: we needed someone to throw off the building.

Adam motioned for us to come over to his computer. "Check this out. I think I've found what we need." Starring back at me from his Mac was something that I hadn't seen since 1982 in the back of a *Penthouse* magazine. It was an inflatable doll. Specifically, Lori the Love Doll.

Adam informed us that he had just ordered her, and that she'd be delivered to us by FedEx tomorrow.

"Do you think it'll work?"

"I hope so. If not, we can always give her as a present at our Christmas party."

The next day the FedEx guy brought in a package for us. As soon as he left, we tore into the box and there she was, in all her deflated plastic glory. Lori had blond plastic hair, two nonblinking eyes, and cherry red lips surrounding a mouth locked into the wide-open position.

The inflation valve was, thank God, on her heel. Adam quickly blew her up. Then he tossed her over to Boone, who bounced her over to me like a very pale beach ball.

"We've got a problem here," I said as I caught her. "She doesn't weigh enough. If there's any wind, she'll blow away. There's no way the firemen will be able to catch her."

"Well, we've got to put clothes on her, that'll weigh her down. We should also get her a wig. That fake hair looks really fake."

"But what about her mouth?" Boone asked, "It's like…wide open."

"C'mon. She's jumping off a building. It'll look like she's screaming," I reasoned.

Another thought we had was that since we were presenting a new TV campaign, we should put the TNT marketing execs in a TV-watching environment. A sterile conference room isn't where most people watch TV. We decided it would be a good idea to outfit their conference room to look like a family room. So they would feel like they were watching TV at home. All we needed was some wood paneling, some popcorn and six recliners. That would be easy.

I had heard about this place called Aaron Rents that rents furniture, so I called their Atlanta store and asked if they rented La-Z-Boy recliners. Not only did they rent them, they delivered. I scheduled them to deliver six recliners to the TNT building by nine a.m. on Thursday. Two hours before our presentation.

The day we left, Boone went to Lowe's and bought ten 4-foot-by-8-foot sheets of wood paneling and loaded them into the van to drive to Atlanta. He crammed them in alongside a disassembled trampoline, a couple bags of fireman suits, and a love doll named Lori. At seven that night we started the four-hour drive to Atlanta.

We laughed on the trip about how nuts we were to start an agency with no cash reserves. We agreed to continue our penny-pinching ways by staying in the cheapest motel we could find.

I slept for six hours, but it seemed like six minutes. We arrived at TNT headquarters with time to spare: a full hour and a half before our presentation. Plenty of time to get set up for our show. Or so we thought.

We checked in and got our TNT visitor badges and met with a guy named Gus, who was in charge of security. We explained to him that we needed to throw something off the roof and that firemen were going to catch it. Shockingly he said, "No problem, I'll show you where we have roof access." We really thought this would be the most difficult part of the whole caper. But this was easy compared to the recliners.

THIS TOOK PLACE IN LATE 2000, ABOUT 10 MONTHS BEFORE 9-11. THERE'S NO WAY WE COULD THROW A BODY OFF THE ROOF OF A TV NETWORK TODAY.

We unloaded our wood paneling from the van and took it up to the fourth floor in the freight elevator. When the doors opened, we saw six giant cardboard boxes in the hallway. We squeezed by them and put the paneling up in the conference room.

Then we realized that the recliners we'd ordered were in those boxes out in the hallway, and they were unassembled.

"Holy God. We've got to put these together."

The meeting was in forty-five minutes. We started ripping the boxes open and taking out the pieces. We borrowed tools from Gus and somehow, someway, we finished assembling the last recliner just as the clock struck eleven. I was sweating like a whore in church when the first marketing person came into the conference room. (I mean, family room.)

Boone walked in a minute later. He had been coordinating the jump with Adam. Adam was up on the roof waiting for the signal to toss Lori. We welcomed everyone into the family room and had them each choose a recliner. Boone served them popcorn and Coke. Then we started.

Forty-five minutes into the presentation, as we were presenting our third campaign, Boone called Adam's cell. Adam then signaled to the "firemen" below, and five seconds later we heard the first, "Step away from the ledge."

Moments later, our doughnut-mouthed friend Lori was hurled to her death.

It took a couple of minutes for the TNT people to realize the whole thing was a stunt.

"You don't get much more dramatic than that!" Greg Johns said to me.

"TNT knows drama. And so does BooneOakley," I crowed.

We had pulled it off. It couldn't have gone better. They loved it and loved us. Now all we had to do was go back home and wait for the call from them telling us that we were TNT's new agency of record.

That call never came.

Sadly, TNT chose Goodby Silverstein. I really shouldn't say sadly. Sad for us I guess, but not for TNT. Goodby won the pitch by proposing a much bigger stunt than throwing a Lori the Love Doll off a building. Goodby told TNT that they should do something dramatic to announce that they were changing the format of their station. Something that would get a ton of press and that everyone would talk about. Goodby told TNT to go off the air. Shut the whole station down for one day. And then do a relaunch as a completely different network.

Now that's drama.

From what I understand, that idea alone won the business. Ironically, Goodby couldn't convince TNT to actually do it. TNT said they couldn't afford to go off the air. They said they would lose too much advertising revenue from shutting down for one day. Oh well. Even though they didn't get to execute that brilliant idea, Goodby completely rebranded TNT's logo and identity, and went on to produce a wildly successful, celebrity-filled campaign. They beat us at our own game. They deserved to win.

If I had been married to Samantha Stephens, I'm sure we would have won. But I'm married to Claire Oakley, and while she's magical in a lot of ways and has given me dozens of campaign ideas over the years, she can't just wiggle her nose and win an account.

But I'd venture to say that I'm still having more fun than Darrin Stephens. Darrin always skipped the Middle Part. He didn't know what he was missing.

HOW WE LANDED THE BIG FISH

SOON AFTER BOONEOAKLEY WON THE CHARLOTTE HORNETS ACCOUNT, I WAS ASKED TO SPEAK ON AN AMERICAN ADVERTISING FEDERATION (AAF) PANEL. The topic was the secret to winning new business, and the panel discussion was entitled "How We Landed The Big Fish."

My panel-mates included an agency president and an agency rainmaker, both of whom had recently landed multimillion-dollar fish. Good, sure, but not as high-profile as the Hornets' business. I prefer quality to quantity when it comes to my fish anyway. Evidently, my role was to give the "creative" perspective on how to win new business.

The presentation was held at a Marriott in Charlotte. It was a luncheon, and as soon as everyone started enjoying their grilled flounder, the moderator introduced the three of us and said, "We'll start with David Oakley from BooneOakley, who just won the Charlotte Hornets account. David, tell us how you landed the big fish."

I walked to the podium and said, "Well, I'm not sure that you'd call the Charlotte Hornets a big fish in terms of billings, especially compared to the size of the accounts these guys are reeling in. They probably would have thrown my fish back."

I started laughing and I think the folks in the room thought I was laughing at my own joke, but the real reason that I was laughing was that I couldn't believe what I was about to do. I was about to demonstrate how to win. I pulled myself together and started talking about new business.

"When you're in a new business presentation, you have to do three things to win. First: you've got to use the right bait. In the case of the Hornets pitch, the bait was smart, strategically sound creative work. But creative alone doesn't win a pitch.

"Second: you have to present it in a way that's memorable. You're pitching against four or five other agencies. So you have to do something that will make the potential client will remember you. But just having them remember you still only gets you to the final round.

"And third: if you truly want to win the pitch, you've got to do something in the presentation that is truly remarkable. Something unforgettable. You have to do something that sticks with them so they'll never forget you."

At that point I looked over at one of the waiters and I said, "I'm kind of hungry. Could you get me a plate?"

"Do you want the flounder?" he asked.

"No, I just want a plate."

"A plate?"

"Yes, just a plate."

He reached over to a stack of plates and handed me one.

"Thank you very much," I said.

I brought the plate back over to the podium and picked up a little container that I'd put there before lunch. The cardboard container was about the size of a cup of soup and said *Live Bait* on the outside.

I looked at the audience eating their flounder and said, "As I said earlier, to catch the big fish, you need the right bait. So on the way here, I stopped at Jimmy's Bait Shop and picked up some fishing worms."

There were a few laughs of disbelief in the crowd. I opened the container and dumped its contents onto the white plate. The fishing worms and dirt made a neat pile of what looked like a wiggly brown pasta and meat sauce.

I held the plate of worms out and walked around room showing everyone that they were real. I must have heard 15 different people shout, "Gross."

"I'll bet you'll remember the guy who came in with the plate of fishing worms, won't you?"

"We'll remember," said a bunch of people, laughing hysterically.

"Just remembering isn't good enough, though. To win, you've got to do something that they will never forget," I said.

I walked back to the podium, held the plate out in front of me and pulled the biggest, fattest fishing worm out of the tangled pile. I held the wiggly worm up high for everyone to see.

"You guys are never going to forget this," I said.

I tilted back my head, opened my mouth, and dropped it down my throat. It squirmed as it went down, and somehow I resisted the urge to retch. I washed it down with a glass of ballroom sweet iced tea.

"Wooooo!" I yelled so loudly Ric Flair would have been jealous. "I don't know about you, but I'm never going to forget that. No matter how hard I try. Thanks for inviting me here today. Enjoy the rest of your lunch." I then returned to my seat and let the other guys follow me.

Eating a fishing worm has never won a new business pitch for us, but it did win over that AAF audience. And winning over the audience is always the key to winning new business.

UNFORTUNATELY...

WE'D GOTTEN ONE OF THOSE CALLS. One of those phone calls that's awesome until the person on the other end speaks the most disappointing word in the English language: *unfortunately*. Nothing good comes after it: "*Unfortunately*, we're awarding our business to another agency."

Moments before, we'd been talking about the Panthers games, full of hope about the young season and eagerly looking forward to working with a new client. "It was a really hard choice and it came down to you guys and another group," the director of marketing said. "We thought you guys were great, but we decided that we should go with an agency that has more category experience."

I'm surprised I remembered a single word after *unfortunately*. We didn't win the pitch. It doesn't matter whether we came in 2nd or

Second place, otherwise known as first loser.

102nd, we still didn't win. As they say in NASCAR, second place is first loser.

I'm a competitive person. I absolutely hate losing. And this one stung more than most. The entire agency had worked endlessly and it was one of the best new business presentations we had ever made.

We came in second. "You guys were a close runner-up," the voice on the other end continued. "It was a hard choice. It was like picking between apples and oranges. You guys are about the big idea. But the other agency had category experience."

I completely tuned out. I was thinking about something that John Adams, the CEO at The Martin Agency, had said to me years ago after we had made a big new business presentation to Alamo Rent A Car. We were packing up the room after our pitch, and I found a leave-behind from the agency (let's call them BCF) that had presented before us. It contained all their creative work and I couldn't wait to see what it was. What it was, was terrible. Their "big idea" was to have Bobby McFerrin sing his hit song, "Don't Worry, Be Happy." But the twist was that they would change the lyrics to "Don't worry, drive happy." I almost puked when I read this.

I was incensed. There was no way we would be beaten by this work. It was horrible. I would be mortified if they picked this campaign over ours.

On the way to the airport, John Adams said to me, "David, I won't be upset at all if we lose to BCF."

"What? Are you kidding me? Of course, you'll be pissed."

"No, I'll be disappointed that we put all this work into it and didn't win, but I won't be upset."

I totally didn't get it.

John went on, "I'd be completely pissed if we lost to an agency whose work I respected. Like Goodby or Wieden or Chiat. But there's no shame in losing if Alamo picks BCF. If they pick BCF, then they aren't the right client for us. They don't want what we do."

That made sense.

When the marketing director called and started with the word *unfortunately*, I knew then that they didn't want what we do. It's that simple. It would be for the best. But it didn't make it any easier to accept.

˙NOT EVERYONE WANTS WHAT WE DO.

The next week we were involved in another pitch. We were competing against four great agencies. *Unfortunately* for those agencies, that time they all came in second.

THE CURSE OF CELINE DION

SOMETIMES YOU GO THROUGH PERIODS OF TIME WHEN IDEAS DON'T COME EASY. No matter what you dream up, you find out it's been done before. When you get in these ruts, you start to feel worthless and insecure. Like a total hack. And the more bad ideas you come up with, the more you doubt yourself. You begin to wonder why. What is it that blocks new ideas from springing from your subconscious? Has someone cast some sort of spell that prevents you from being brilliant? Definitely maybe.

I was going through one of these periods a couple of years ago. It was a major creative slump. It was depressing. As I often do when I find myself in one of those times, I thought about good ideas that we had in the past and wondered why we couldn't come up with shit now. I found myself reminiscing about a campaign that we did for a Charlotte radio station—one of my all-time favorites.

It was 1999, and instead of Prince, every radio station in the country was playing "My Heart Will Go On," the theme song from the film Titanic. I absolutely hated that song. And I hated Celine Dion for singing it. It was everywhere. On the hip-hop stations. On the country stations. At gas stations. I couldn't even pump gas in peace. And of course, in elevators. But at least that made sense.

That summer, we were asked by 106.5 The End, an alternative rock station, to create an ad campaign to drive listeners to their end of the dial. The station manager, Jack Daniel, gave us complete creative freedom. We could do most anything we wanted, even use images of the musicians whose songs 106.5 played. We could put Pearl Jam, U2, R.E.M., and Nine Inch Nails in our ads if we wanted. What a plum assignment!

We started knocking around some ideas using Michael Stipe and Trent Reznor. They were pretty cool. The images were fantastic. But we realized this was exactly what every other radio station did in their ads. They showed pictures of musicians and had head-lines like *Where Bono Rocks*, or *Where R.E.M. Rolls, 97.9 FM*. Pretty lame stuff.

> JACK DANIEL IS ONE OF THE NAMES IN THE BOOK THAT I DIDN'T CHANGE. IT'S THE GUY'S REAL NAME. JACK'S A GREAT GUY. IF HE HAD BEEN A DOUCHE, I WOULD HAVE CHANGED HIS NAME TO JIM BEAM.

Then we had another thought. What if we made fun of the music that other stations played? We could say who 106.5 *was* by saying who they *weren't*. We could make fun of any type of music that was being spun on the popular and easy listening stations. There were so many targets at that time: Hanson, Garth Brooks, Spice Girls. And of course, Celine Dion. I hated Celine Dion. I hated that song.

When I wrote the line, *We Wish Celine Dion Had Been on the Titanic*, I meant it. And when I showed it to Boone, I knew we had a winner.

"That's kind of mean," he said.

"Yes it is," I said. "But it's from the heart. The best headlines come from the heart."

We decided to make the billboards look like old jukebox labels, with the musician's name in the middle and the two songs on top and bottom: "We Wish" was on the top line, "Celine Dion" was in the middle, and "Had Been On The Titanic," was on the bottom.

We wrote some more lines, including *We'll play Hanson if you'll*

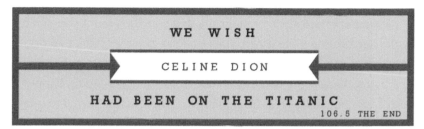

How could anyone wish that Celine had drowned before she recorded her hit song? (I guess I'm not really as nice as Sweeney said in my foreword.)

clean up the vomit, and *What came first: Spice Girls or the mute button?* But the Celine ad was my favorite. I hated her. We comped them up and took them over to 106.5.

Jack Daniel read the Celine line and howled. "After hearing that song 400 million times this summer, I don't think anyone in the country would disagree." Then he said my three favorite words from a client: "Let's do it." Soon the campaign was all over Charlotte.

Apparently Jack was a bit off in his estimation of how many people were sick of Celine. A lot of people liked her. No. A lot of people *loved* her. And I think every single one of them called 106.5 to protest, which created a ton of buzz for 106.5. Soon after the ad ran, they became Charlotte's #1 radio station, proving again that there's no such thing as bad publicity.

The campaign did a lot for 106.5. But it did even more for us It won a ton of awards, including a Clio, a national ADDY, and two One Show Pencils. At the One Show Award ceremony, Sally Hogshead gave us a shout-out, saying that "The Celine ad is the my favorite ad in the show. It's hilarious." That year, *Creativity* magazine named Boone and me "Hot Creative Team." I got job offers from Fallon and Wieden+Kennedy. Making fun of Celine was very good for my career.

But not long after, I started to feel a little twinge of guilt. Not so much that it stopped me from collecting the hardware, mind you, but I started to question what we had done.

My parents had always taught me that you don't build yourself up by putting other people down. But that was exactly what I had done. I had never met Celine Dion. Who was I to say that the world would be a better place if she had drowned before she recorded that song? I don't know where this feeling came from, but it really started to gnaw at me.

Maybe Celine is a really nice and caring person. I had completely benefited by being mean to her. I started thinking how *I* would feel if someone wrote an ad about me that said they wished I were dead. Was I getting soft or just going crazy?

I brushed the thought off and returned to the reality of this horrible creative slump that I was mired in. Why in the world couldn't I come up with a good idea? What was causing this rut? I paused for a second and then my mouth dropped wide open.

It's Celine, I thought. *Oh my God.*

We hadn't had a huge idea in a long time. Come to think of it, we hadn't won a One Show Pencil since we won for the Celine board. Had we inadvertently jinxed ourselves?

The Boston Red Sox suffered under "the Curse of the Bambino" for eighty-five years. The Chicago Cubs have been under "the Curse of the Billy Goat" since the 1940s.

Could we have fallen victim to "the Curse of Celine"?

That was it. That was the only explanation possible.

There was only one thing that was going to break this slump: I had to make things right with Celine.

I needed to go see her perform, the sooner the better. I went online and saw that she was performing nightly at Caesars Palace in Las Vegas. I had a new-business trip to Vegas scheduled later that month and I vowed to make Celine a part of it.

The next two weeks dragged by as we prepared for our presentation, but finally John Boone, Demian Brink, Phil Smith, and I flew to Vegas. As soon as we landed, we rented a car and drove to our meeting outside of Vegas with an energy drink manufacturer. We figured if the meeting didn't go well, at least we had two nights in Vegas immediately after to blow off a little steam. The slump continued in the meeting. We sucked, and besides, the client wasn't someone we really wanted to work with. We made a beeline for the MGM Grand, checked into our rooms, and met downstairs to commence partying. A night of blackjack and Budweiser ensued.

After about four hours of sleep, it was already the next afternoon. I still hadn't told Phil, Boone, or Demian about my theory on the Celine Curse—or my plan for remedial action. We met at MGM Studio Café for brunch and Demian asked if we were interested in going to Blue Man Group that evening. Boone said that he was in. Demian then looked at me and asked, "What about you, Oaks?"

"Uhmmm…I've got plans tonight."

"Plans? What plans?"

"He's probably planning on losing some more money," Phil interjected.

"Not exactly. I'm going to the Celine Dion show tonight."

"Celine Dion?!" Demian replied, laughing so hard he almost choked on his huevos rancheros.

"But you hate Celine," Boone said.

"No I don't. I don't know her well enough to hate her. Besides, it's hard to explain, but I owe her."

"You owe it to Celine Dion to spend $125 to see her show?" Demian countered.

"Well, yeah. I feel like it will in some way repay her for using her name in that ad."

"Dude, you are crazy," said Phil.

"Well, it's just something that I've gotta do."

They laughed at me, wondering what on earth had gotten into me.

I left them at MGM and walked over to the box office at Caesars Palace and asked the lady there about getting tickets to see Celine. She laughed at me too. "Celine's been sold out for months. She's only doing the show for two more weeks."

"Do you have any single tickets?

"Nope. Sold out."

"Hey," said the lady at the next ticket booth. "Stop back by later this afternoon. Sometimes people cancel their reservations."

"Not for this show," my ticket lady said. "But check back anyway. What have you got to lose?"

What I had to lose was my chance to shake the Curse of Celine. So I followed her advice and checked back a couple of hours later. "Do you have any tickets for tonight's show?" I asked my box office friend.

She typed something into her computer and said, "I don't believe this."

"What?"

"Four tickets just came available for tonight's show."

"Cool," I said feeling lucky. "How much?"

"$125 each. In a private box."

"I'll take one, please."

"One?" she asked indignantly.

"Yeah, one. I'm by myself."

"Do you know how much these are going for on eBay?"

"Tell me."

"$1200 each. Are you sure you just want one?"

OK, now this was a moral dilemma. The reason I was going to see Celine was to make up for my perceived trespass against her. I wanted to set things right between the two of us. If I were to profit from my atonement, the Curse of Celine would not only haunt me for the rest of my life, but probably my descendants too. On the other hand, I reasoned with myself, I'm a business man. I could sell the three other tickets for $3600. It would be by far the easiest and most money I had ever made in Vegas. I stood there thinking for what seemed like an eternity.

"No, I'll just take one."

"Suit yourself," she replied with a roll of the eyes.

Eight o'clock rolled around and I went back to Caesars Palace to see the show. It was quite the scene. Everyone was dressed to the nines. Apparently seeing Celine was the highlight of some people's lives. I was still wearing shorts and a T-shirt. I started eavesdropping on the conversation between two women waiting to get inside the theater.

"I just love Celine."

"Me too. She's the perfect woman."

"Did you see her on Oprah?"

"She and Oprah are like soul mates."

"Oprah is real picky about her soul mates."

"She's only got three: Stedman, Gayle King, and Celine."

I thought, *Thank God I'm here to ask for forgiveness. Being on Celine's shit list is one thing. Being on Oprah's is a whole different ballgame.*

The usher led me to my box seat. And what a seat it was: a full on La-Z-Boy recliner with cup holders, and carpet that didn't stick to your feet. I couldn't believe my luck. I certainly wasn't anticipating a mosh pit, but this was an unexpected heaven. I had been partying big time in Vegas and the thought of being totally stretched out for this show was quite appealing. I plopped down into that mass of comfort and pushed the lever on the side of the chair, which lifted my feet to a nice elevated position. My sight line for the stage was perfect. I could feel the curse lifting. When Celine came out, she'd be right above my feet. This was awesome.

The next thing I remember was someone hitting me hard on the shoulder. I looked up and saw a lady sitting in the recliner next to me.

"Sir…sir, you're snoring."

"Huh? What?"

"You've been doing it the entire show."

"Sorry, sorry," I groggily apologized.

Then I heard the first note of the *Titanic* song. I felt chills over my entire body. I'm not sure if it was the song or because I had been asleep in an air-conditioned theater for an hour and a half in shorts and a T-shirt.

It was the grand finale of the show.

Celine started singing, *"Every night in my dreams, I see you, I feel you, that is how I know you go on…"*

In my well-rested and almost dreamlike state, Celine looked angelic, serenading me with the ultimate song of love and devotion.

Celine's voice was an instrument like I'd never heard. It was incredible. My contempt for her melted like a North Atlantic iceberg in the Mojave dessert. She hit the high notes much better than Ana Gasteyer on *Saturday Night Live*. And her awkward spidery-armed dance moves were sincere and completely endearing.

When the song ended, Celine left the stage to a thunderous ovation. I wanted more. But I had really gotten what I had come for. A bond had formed between Celine and me. And the way she sang that song to me, I knew that all was forgiven. I had a new love and respect for her, and I knew that it would go on and on.

But the Curse of Celine would not.

Soon after this trip, BooneOakley hatched one of our best ideas ever.

THERE'S ALWAYS FOX

I HAD A DREAM ABOUT DOGS. It wasn't a man's-best-friend type of dream. I dreamed about dogs fucking. Maybe they were making love, but I'd say they were just plain fucking. They were going at it in a cheap hotel room. It was a scene straight out of a porn movie. And yes, they were doing it doggie-style.

When I opened my eyes and looked at the ceiling, I thought, *That was weird.* Then I exclaimed, "That's it! That is it!" I jumped out of bed, grabbed a notepad, and started writing a script.

We had been working on an assignment for the Humane Society of Charlotte for about a month. My friend Trip Park had told me that he was friends with the marketing director at the Humane Society. They needed help getting the word out about their organization, and he thought BooneOakley was the perfect agency to make that happen. They didn't have much money, but they wanted something that would break through the clutter. Get them noticed. (That's pretty much the same thing that every client says, by the way.) Trip also said he thought I'd like his friend.

So I met with Catherine Page, the marketing director, at the Humane Society office. Their office was actually the dog pound. She took me around and showed me the dogs that were up for adoption that day. There were so many. It was clear that they were operating on a shoestring budget. She told me about the problem with the over-population of dogs and cats in Mecklenburg County, and that over eight thousand dogs and cats were euthanized every month in the

Charlotte region. She believed this problem could be helped with an advertising campaign that informed people about how important it was to spay or neuter their pets.

Trip was right. I instantly liked Catherine. And since the BooneOakley mantra is "Do Great Work for People You Like," we decided to take on the project pro bono.

"DO GREAT WORK FOR PEOPLE YOU LIKE

We worked on the assignment for a couple of weeks and had some pretty good ideas. We were scheduled to present them on Friday afternoon. I literally had the dream the morning of the meeting.

When we got to her office, Catherine introduced us to Beverly Watts, the president of the Humane Society. Catherine had told me a bit about Beverly at our earlier meeting. She was seventy-three years old and old-school Charlotte. So naturally, I pictured her to be a Myers Park society matron. A prig in pearls with iron-gray hair that wouldn't budge in a blizzard.

But Beverly wasn't like I imagined. She was tall and trim and had slightly unkempt hair. She was wearing funky jewelry and her eyes seemed to be laughing. But still, I couldn't believe that I was about to try to sell a seventy-three-year-old woman a porn film starring two dogs. That takes balls.

To be safe, we brought a couple of other ideas. Ideas we felt sure they would buy. But the late-breaking doggie porn idea was clearly the best in breed.

We named the spot "Puppy Love." The name was a bit misleading, but it seemed a little more buyable than "Doggie Style." We decided to show "Puppy Love" first.

Catherine and Beverly led us into a conference room, which was furnished with what can only be described as Salvation Army rejects.

The Humane Society is a humble place. Beverly was holding a skinny, trembling beagle that had been rescued the day before.

"This idea is called 'Puppy Love,'" I said as I began my pitch. "We open in a cheap hotel room. There are two dogs relaxing, side by side, under the covers of a bed with their heads on the pillows. The male dog starts nuzzling his nose on the female dog's neck. The female looks at him and, feeling a little frisky, gets out from under the covers and stands on all fours. We cut to the male dog's face. He looks very happy. He gets out from under the covers and starts to mount the female dog from behind. She pushes him off and motions with her head to the bedside table. We cut to a close up of the table and on it is a condom. The male dog goes to the table and eats the condom. The female nods approvingly. We cut back to the pair humping. Cut to final art card: 'Dogs don't understand birth control. Have your dog spayed or neutered.'"

"Oh my God," Beverly exclaimed. "Oh my God!"

Catherine looked at her and then at us and then back at Beverly.

I wasn't sure what Beverly's reaction really was. Did she hate it? Was she appalled?

"This is exactly what we need. It's awesome!" Beverly exclaimed.

"Well, we asked you to do something to get people talking. This will get people talking," Catherine added.

I couldn't believe what I was hearing. We left the safer ideas in the portfolio case.

Now we had to figure out a way to get it produced. On a $5000 budget. We sent the storyboard to our friend Peter Darley Miller, a fantastic director who had shot several spots for us in the past. Normally, his fee alone was ten times the Humane Society's budget.

Peter called about five minutes after he got the storyboard.

"I *have* to shoot this spot. It's ridiculously good and I've always wanted to do a porno."

He talked with Frank Stiefel, owner of Stiefel & Co. Productions.

Frank said, "If you guys can get out to LA, we'll shoot it for you."

We flew to LA. Since we had no budget for a location shoot—or the rental of a cheap motel room—we shot the spot in an office at Stiefel & Co. We removed the desk from an empty office and replaced it with a bed and side table. We hung a thrift store painting above the bed and *voilà*, we had ourselves a cheap hotel room. Peter asked a friend of his who was a dog trainer if he would bring a couple of his dogs and have them act in our spot. He agreed, and the next day, we were shooting.

It didn't take much directing or training to get a male and female dog to do what they do. Buster and Trixie were naturals. Within an hour, we had every shot that we wanted. But the dog eating the condom wasn't as funny in person as it had been on the storyboard.

Peter had an idea: "Why don't we put the condom on his tail?"

Condoms don't make many guys smile, but I was grinning ear to ear. Buster had a four-inch stump of a tail. I quickly unrolled a condom over it. Peter yelled, "Action."

As soon as Buster mounted Trixie his tail wagged so hard the condom almost flew off. The entire set exploded in laughter. We got the shot in only one take. So did Buster. I knew right then we had something special.

The Humane Society now had a great TV spot. But no media budget. This didn't bother Catherine Page at all. She did a segment each Wednesday on WBTV, the Charlotte CBS affiliate, promoting the Humane Society. Catherine brought puppies and cats for adoption onto the noon newscast. She said there was no question that they would run a Humane Society spot. She scheduled a meeting to show them the spot.

I was feeling confident when we went in to meet with Mary McMillan, the general manager of WBTV. I was really proud of the spot and believed it would make a difference. Mary welcomed us to her Emmy-filled office with a big smile. We cued up the new commercial and pressed play. I watched Mary's face as her inviting expression shifted into a slack jaw in exactly thirty seconds.

"Well, that's some commercial," Mary said. "It's well-produced. Beautifully produced. But...but honestly, there is no way in the world that we are going to air that on WBTV. I'm really sorry, Catherine, but this is not the type of image that we want to project to our audience. This is a family TV station. We are

I don't think this is what Donny Osmond called Puppy Love.

big supporters of the Humane Society. But we cannot support this. I'm sorry."

Mary said that WBTV would continue to air the Humane Society's segment every Wednesday, and would be happy to air a public service commercial for them. But not this commercial.

I was bummed, embarrassed, and I felt horrible for Catherine. We had sold them on an idea that would never see the light of day. An idea they had spent $5000 to produce. I know that they had gotten a bargain on producing the spot, but it was their entire marketing budget. They could have spayed and neutered a lot of dogs for five grand.

We walked out of Mary's office and down the hallway toward the front door. Catherine and I said nothing to each other. It was a total walk of shame. I felt like I had my tail between my legs. With a condom on it.

As we walked through the lobby, Catherine put her arm around me and said, "Don't worry, David. There's always FOX."

"What?" I asked.

"Don't worry about it. We'll go to FOX tomorrow."

I couldn't believe she wasn't upset.

The next morning, Catherine and I were sitting in the lobby of FOX Charlotte, waiting to meet with John Hutchinson, the general manager, and Jeff Arrowood, the program director. The flat-screen on the wall behind the receptionist played the FOX show that was currently on the air. It was *The Jerry Springer Show*. Today's topic: tickle fetishes.

"Wow, if they'll air that, they might just air this," I said to Catherine.

"I think we've got a shot."

We showed the spot to Mr. Hutchinson and Mr. Arrowood.

"That's quite a spot you've got there, Catherine," said Mr. Hutchinson.

"Thank you, Mr. Hutchinson. These guys did a great job on it."

"They sure did. Call me Hutch. Have you showed it to anyone else?

"Well, truthfully, we showed it to WBTV yesterday," Catherine said.

"How'd that go?

"They refused to air it," I blurted out.

"Really?" Hutchinson said with a sly smile.

"WBTV thought it would 'upset their viewing audience.'"

"Well WCCB is not WBTV. Tell ya what: we're not only going to air it, we're going to make it our lead story on the news tonight. This is much more than a public service announcement. This is news."

Mr. Hutchinson was a man of his word.

All afternoon, teasers for the evening news aired on FOX showing a clip from "Puppy Love" with the voiceover: *A provocative new ad campaign from the Humane Society of Charlotte. Have they gone too far? Breaking news at six.*

On the newscast, FOX showed the entire spot, and the WCCB reporter interviewed people who had seen it. They encouraged viewers to go to their website and vote in an online poll: effective or over-the-top?

The next morning, the *Charlotte Observer* ran a story about the controversial Humane Society spot that was banned from WBTV. They interviewed Beverly Watts and asked if she was proud of putting out a message that many folks deemed obscene. Her response was brilliant: "You know what's really obscene? Euthanizing more than 100,000 dogs and cats every year in Mecklenburg County. That's obscene."

Donations to the Humane Society tripled that fall, and our "Puppy Love" spot went on to win more than its share of awards.

I never would have dreamed that this little ad would cause such a commotion in the ad world. That's because I don't dream about advertising. I dream about dogs fucking.

PING-PONG

WHENEVER I GET STUCK FOR AN IDEA OR HAVE WRITER'S BLOCK, I PLAY PING-PONG. It's a simple game and anyone can play. It takes a lot of practice to play well, but playing well isn't the object. The object is to give your mind a break. To let go of the deadlines and bad ideas and just concentrate on hitting that feather-light ball back to your opponent. Thirty minutes of Ping-Pong is therapeutic.

Some people say fish is brain food. I think Ping-Pong is idea food. Playing Ping-Pong stimulates creativity. Every ad agency should have a table. In fact, every business should have one.

Not long ago, we were working on a new business pitch, and we had seen a couple of rounds of work from our creative teams. We had seen a lot of ideas, but not a lot of good ideas. Maybe we were asking too much of our teams, putting too much pressure on them because we felt like we absolutely had to win this account. Then it hit me what the problem was: We were working without a source of idea nourishment. We didn't have a Ping-Pong table anymore.

We had always had one, but for some reason, we'd gotten rid of ours a few months earlier during a big clean-up day at BooneOakley. Granted, it had seen better days. It had a huge crack across the top and one of its legs was broken. But when that table left BooneOakley, our mojo went with it. Now we needed it back. Immediately.

I figured I could get a new Ping-Pong table at Dick's Sporting Goods, so I went back to my office and logged on to their site. I was shocked: a decent Ping-Pong table ran around 500 bucks.

We simply couldn't afford that. Not now anyway. We had just lost an account and had to lay off several employees. Morale wasn't great at the agency, and the last thing we needed was our people complaining about not being able to afford a print producer and a designer, but we could drop half a grand on a game. But I knew that we needed one. A Ping-Pong table was part of our DNA and we needed some ideas.

Hmmm, I thought, *maybe I could find one on Craigslist.* Sure enough, after ten minutes of surfing, I found one. It sounded almost too good to be true. "Brand new Stiga Pro Ping-Pong table. $75 bucks. You pick it up, in Troutman."

I called the number listed and a woman with a thick western North Carolina accent answered. I told her that I was interested in the Ping-Pong table. She said she had several of them, but I'd have to pick it up. Troutman is about forty-five minutes north of Charlotte.

"If I come pick it up this afternoon, can I have it for $50?" I asked.

She thought about it for a minute and said, "Yeah, if you get it before three o'clock."

I looked at my watch and saw that it was one thirty, and said, "It's a deal. See you in about an hour."

Yes! I'm getting this table for 10 percent of what it costs at Dick's. Now all I need is a truck. I went straight to Kathryn Bolles' office. Kathryn owns several horses and drives a big-ass Chevy truck.

"Hey Kathryn, any chance I could borrow your truck for a couple of hours?"

She looked at me inquisitively, and asked, "Sure, but what are you up to?"

"I just bought a Ping-Pong table on Craigslist and I want to go pick it up. Can I borrow it?"

"Sure," she said, and handed me her keys.

Five minutes later I was rolling north on I-77. It was a clear spring day, the road was traffic-free, so I put the windows down and I cranked the first song that came on the radio, the Stones: *"You can't always get what you want, but if you try sometimes you get what you need."*

I couldn't help but think how appropriate this song was. I wanted a big idea and it wasn't happening. Now I was getting what I needed. And what the agency needed: a Ping-Pong table. I knew that a big idea wouldn't be far behind. I love when stuff like this happens.

The last ten miles took me closer and closer to the middle of nowhere. I knew that I was getting close when the woman's directions had me turn on a dirt road. I followed the winding gravel road for three-quarters of a mile. I saw the numbers 1122 on the mailbox. About two hundred yards from the road sat a nondescript brick ranch house, not unlike thousands that had been built in subdivisions across the south in the 1970s. But this was on several acres of land. I took a right and drove in. There was a low muddy spot halfway to the house with three muddy Ping-Pong tabletops lying across the driveway. It was as if a stately gentleman had laid his coat across a mud puddle so a lady could safely step over. I drove over them and parked my truck beside the house. I hopped out, skipped up the front steps and rang the doorbell.

A cacophony of deafening barks ensued. I jumped away from the door. The scratching, clawing, and baritone yelping made the hair on the back of my neck stand straight up.

I looked over at the picture window and saw two Doberman pinschers and a pit bull jumping on a couch with their front paws on the window, licking their chops between barks. From the sound of things, there must have been ten more behind the door.

I quickly backed away down the front steps, turned and ran back to my truck. I slammed the door behind me and pulled out my cell phone. I took a deep breath and called the number from Craigslist. It rang a few times and then I heard her voice: *"Hi, this is Tina. We ain't home right now..."*

Damn it. I drove all the way up here and she isn't even home.

Right about then I saw a small cloud of dust in the distance. It was a truck speeding down the gravel road toward me. Before it got to the driveway, it veered sharply to the right and bounced over the shallow roadside ditch. It continued barreling across the front yard, heading right for my truck. The driver locked the brakes and brought the truck to a skidding halt, *Dukes of Hazzard*–style, right in front of the house, about twenty feet from me. The driver's door flung open and a man jumped out. He pulled his baseball cap low over his brow and a moment later started pointing at me. "Hey! Hey!" he shouted as he strode toward my truck with a purpose. That purpose, no doubt, was to kick my ass.

I grabbed the camouflage Red Man baseball cap that was on Kathryn's front seat and quickly put it on. I'm not sure why. It was an instinctive move. Maybe it would be harder for him to kill a fellow redneck than some surfer dude.

"What are you doing here?" he yelled as he strode toward me.

Oh my God, I thought. *This guy thinks I'm banging his girlfriend.*

"I came to get a Ping-Pong table." My voice cracked like a thirteen-year-old Peter Brady's.

"Oh..." he said as he starred at my face from about three feet away. "You're the dude who talked to Tina. That's my girlfriend. She stays here sometimes and feeds the dogs."

"Yeah, I spoke with Tina on the phone."

"I didn't know who you were. I don't like drivin' up to my house and seeing another man there. Know what I mean?"

"Oh yeah," I said, trying to be as cool as possible.

"Shut up!" he yelled right in my face. But he was directing his anger at his dogs, who were still barking. "Them dogs are driving me crazy."

"They scared the shit out of me when I rang the doorbell."

"You rang the doorbell? It's a wonder they didn't bust through the picture window and eat your ass up."

"Yeah, they sounded hungry. How many are in there?"

"Fourteen or fifteen, depending on whether Tina took her pit bull puppy home. There's six pits, four Dobermans, three, no, two German shepherds, and two mutts."

"They always stay in the house?"

"Yeah, and they's tore it all to hell."

"Bummer. Well, I'm David Oakley. I drove up here to get a Ping-Pong table. You got one?"

"Yeah, I got a bunch of 'em. I'm Keith Jones. Good to meet ya."

I uneasily got out of the truck and shook his hand.

"C'mon down here to my basement," he said as he started walking down the hill toward the back of his house.

I followed him a couple of steps and then instinctively stopped. *What the hell am I doing? Following Jeffrey Dahmer's cousin into his basement? All to save a couple hundred dollars? I must be completely insane.*

When he reached the basement door, he turned and saw that I wasn't right behind him.

"What are you waitin' on? C'mon," he said with a grin that revealed that his girlfriend was not a dental hygienist. He was missing one of his eye teeth and it looked like a couple more would be going to the tooth fairy soon.

This guy's on something. Meth, probably, I thought. For a second, I considered making a run for my truck and getting the hell out of there. But instead, I kept walking. I had driven that far, and I wanted a Ping-Pong table. I wasn't going back empty-handed.

"No-Teeth" Keith opened the door and I followed him in. He flipped on the light and closed the door behind us. He turned and locked his glassy eyes with mine. He squinted as if to get a better look at me, paused, and said, "I'm not on drugs, you know."

"Ah, I didn't think so."

"I'm not on drugs," he repeated.

Nothing says, "Hey I'm on drugs!" like a guy saying he's not on drugs. This may have been the most frightened I've ever been in my life. *Hmmm,* I thought, *maybe going back empty-handed was better than not going back at all. I've got to find a way out of here.*

I looked around the basement. It was a cornucopia of weirdness. Five creepy-looking plastic snowmen glared at me as I tried to change the conversation. "Why do you have four freezers down here?"

"I keep dead bodies in 'em." Keith started laughing like it was the best joke he'd ever heard. He must have seen the sheer terror in my eyes, so he clarified what he was saying. "Deer bodies. Venison. I'm a hunter. You're a hunter, aren't ya?"

"Ah...no."

"Well, why are you wearing that camo cap?"

"Cause I'm hunting a Ping-Pong table."

"Well, I've got about fifteen of 'em right over here." And there against the far wall, behind a couple of completely decorated Christmas trees, was a stack of Stiga Ping-Pong tabletops. They were unassembled and not in boxes. Beside them was a pile of Ping-Pong nets, a neat stack of aluminum table legs, and a box full of various screws and bolts to put them together.

"Let me pick you out a good set." And he started picking out the pieces that I needed. "Let's see, you need four legs, a couple of these cross braces, and of course, you need a net." He searched through an old cardboard box, looked up and said, "You came all the way up from Charlotte, I'll throw in a package of balls."

He handed them to me. "Hey, thanks, that's really nice."

"OK, that's everything. Let's take this stuff up to your truck."

He walked over to the door and tried to turn the doorknob. It didn't turn. He slowly looked around to me and said, "We're locked in." I didn't say anything. I just stared at him. Then he burst into a hyena laugh and said, "I'm messing with you," and opened the door.

We carried everything up to the truck and got it all loaded. I gave him $50 in cash. I climbed into the driver's seat and closed the door, then rolled the window down and thanked him.

He leaned against the door and asked, "Where are you going use this table? In your bonus room or something?"

"No, I'm taking it to our office."

"Your *office*? No one will ever get any work done."

I smiled and said, "That's what everybody thinks."

As I pulled out of the driveway, I looked at Keith in my rearview mirror and realized I'd barely been breathing for the last fifteen minutes. I let out a big guffaw in relief and considered that it was pretty weird that Keith had a basement full of Ping-Pong tables. But I didn't really care where they'd come from. I drove home, knowing that soon, not only would we be getting some work done, we'd be getting some *great* work done.

NEED A GREAT AD? JUST LIE, A LITTLE...

SOMETIMES ALL IT TAKES TO PULL OFF A GREAT ADVERTISING STUNT IS A LITTLE WHITE LIE. More often than not, though, it takes more than one. The muffin billboard caper we pulled off for Bloom supermarkets is a prime example.

It was a good billboard: a silver muffin pan with six muffins in it, held by an oven mitt. The headline read, *Jumbo Muffins: Always in Bloom.*

A headline less than eight words? Check. An eye-catching visual? Check. Was the type legible? Check. It was a good billboard. One that people would notice and, more than likely, one that would influence people to shop at Bloom.

It was good. But it wasn't good enough. It needed something extra. Something unexpected. Something that would capture people's attention and give them something to talk about. Better yet, give them something to lie about.

What if one of the muffins fell off and crushed a car? A car

On its own, this was a good billboard.

that was innocently parked beneath the billboard. That would be memorable. Yeah, that would be unforgettable. But next to impossible to pull off. Could we make it happen? We could give it a shot.

That's how the Bloom muffin board started. We had a good billboard idea, but we weren't satisfied with good.

■ "GOOD IS THE ENEMY OF GREAT."
—JAY CHIAT

We called Gale Bonnell at Adams Outdoor. She said she loved the creative and would do anything to help us get it produced. We told her that we wanted a board near a Bloom supermarket. She said there was one on Highway 150 near the Bloom in Mooresville. It was beside a Shell station. There was a spot right beneath the board where we could park a car. But why would there be a car parked beneath the board? Because the car would be for sale. We'd put a For Sale sign in the window. That would explain why the car was sitting there for a week.

Next we had to get a car. Mark Bartlett, the operations manager at Adams, told me he knew where to find one. We met him and he took us to a junkyard. There we bought a dark brown Kia Sephia for $200. It didn't run, but we didn't need it to run. He loaded it onto the back of an Adams truck and we took it back to Adams. I told Mark I thought we really wanted a red car so people would notice it. "Don't worry about it, David," Mark told me. "I'll paint it."

A few days later I stopped by Adams, and sure enough, we had a red Kia. It looked like new. It didn't run, but it looked good. It was a shame we had to crush it.

The muffins were there as well. They were definitely jumbo: six of them, each the size of a sea turtle. They looked delicious even though they were made of Styrofoam with a glaze of acrylic paint.

The next day, Mark and his men put the billboard up. I went with them and put a For Sale sign on the windshield of the Kia. I bought a prepaid cell phone and put the phone number on the driver's-side window. I then recorded a voicemail greeting on the cell phone. "Hi, you've reached Vern. If you are calling about the red Kia that I have for sale, please leave me a message and I'll get right back to you."

Phase One had begun. Now all we had to do was wait a week and it would be time for a muffin to fall.

The day before the muffin drop, I got a call from Robin Johnson, our main client at Bloom. She was very excited about the muffin caper and in fact was the one who approved the idea. She was calling to tell me that the in-house PR guy at Food Lion, Bloom's parent company, loved the idea and was insisting that he call the *Charlotte Observer* and tip them off to what was happening ahead of time. He said he had a long-standing relationship with the editor that would be ruined if he didn't give the *Observer* the scoop on this story. I couldn't believe what I was hearing. If we had a reporter there, it wouldn't look like an accident. The element of surprise would be gone, and all of our efforts wasted. It was a horrible idea.

"You gotta talk him out of this," I practically begged. "Is there anything you can do to get him to understand?"

"I'll think of something," Robin said, as she hung up. She wasn't very convincing.

Twenty-four hours later, it was time for the muffin to drop. Our plan was simple. Arrive at two a.m., in the cover of darkness when no one was around. We would remove one of the muffins from the billboard and replace it with a vinyl patch that looked like the bottom of a muffin pan. Then we'd smash the top of the car, place the muffin on it and leave. Mark figured we'd be done in two hours, tops.

Everything went smoothly. A fifty-foot extendable cherry picker lifted Mark up onto the catwalk of the billboard. The muffin was not a problem to remove. The vinyl patch was easily attached to the bill-board. It looked like a muffin had just slipped out of it. Now all we had to do was smash the Kia and we'd be outta there. That's where the smooth sailing ended.

Mark got one of his guys to hit the top of the car with a sledge-hammer. It made a couple of dents, but nothing like what we were looking for. We wanted the entire roof to look like it had caved in from the weight of the muffin. Mark climbed on top of the car and jumped up and down. Nothing. He then walked away toward the Adams crane truck. He told one of his guys to get a chain and attach it to a ten-foot section of steel pipe. The same pipe they used as a main support on a billboard.

The crane lifted the two-ton pipe high in the air. It dangled about fifteen feet above the Kia. "OK, drop it!" Mark yelled. The pipe hurled down toward the car. But instead of a smashing crash, the pipe bounced off the roof, barely denting the top of the car. "Damn, that's one tough car." They lifted the pipe up again, even higher, and dropped it from thirty feet above the car. Same result: big bounce, small dent.

"We gotta think of something else."

"It's the damn I-beam," Mark said with more than a hint of frus-tration. I learned that night that all passenger cars have a safety feature that keeps the cabin from collapsing if the car ever flips. Even Kias. "We'll have to cut it. Do we have a saw that will cut steel?" Mark asked one of his assistants.

The time kept ticking. By now it was 5:20 a.m. Only about forty-five minutes before daylight. We had to get the roof to collapse.

The next thing that I knew, sparks were flying everywhere. Mark had jerry-rigged an electric saw and was cutting through the I-beam. He cut it on both sides and then dropped the pipe one more time. This time the roof collapsed, shattering both the windshield and the back window.

Now all we had to do was put the muffin on top. We lifted the Styrofoam muffin and put it into place. Mark drilled a hole in the roof and started bolting the muffin to the car. I thought this was a waste of time. If the muffin were attached, it would be obvious that this was a fake. Mark insisted that if we didn't attach it, the muffin would be stolen the first night. He twisted his wrench one last time. "That'll do it. Let's get out of here."

We threw all of our stuff into the Adams Outdoor truck, hopped in, and rolled out of there at dawn's first light.

I've often heard that criminals return to the scene of the crime. Maybe that's why we couldn't resist coming back a few minutes later and parking our cars across the street. It was a great vantage point to watch the festivities.

A fallen muffin and a crushed Kia elevated this billboard from good to great.

It was a rubbernecking parade. Highway 150 was jammed with rush-hour traffic. But no one seemed to be in a great hurry to get to work. Car after car turned into the Shell station that morning. No one was getting gas. They were just taking pictures.

Those who weren't taking pictures were having pictures taken of them.

"I saw it fall," a lady wearing a Rusty Wallace NASCAR shirt said to the reporter from WSOC-TV. "Fell right on that red car. Crushed it. About seven o'clock this morning. The windows busted out and glass went everywhere. Luckily there was no one else around."

The attendant at the Shell station said, "I heard a crash and thought it was a wreck. I walked outside and saw that muffin on the car. It was the damnedest thing I've ever seen."

Tony Cioffi and Gale Bonnell from Adams Outdoor pulled up beside us to watch. The two of them took the caper up another notch. "We just stopped by Bloom. We bought every muffin that they had. Now they're sold out," Tony said, and grinned.

"Wow, that is one effective billboard."

Robin Johnson and Angie Hunter, our clients at Bloom, came by to see the board a few minutes later. The first thing Robin said was, "This is freaking awesome. Did you hear that some guy that saw the billboard had stopped at Bloom an hour ago and bought every muffin that we had?"

Our clients were psyched. We were psyched. And the guys from Adams Outdoor were psyched. We high-fived all around.

I then remembered the PR guy from Food Lion so I asked Robin, "How did you convince the PR guy not to call the newspaper ahead of time?"

Robin smiled and said, "I just told him that the muffin wasn't falling until next week."

"Brilliant, Robin," I smiled and said, "To make things happen, sometimes you just gotta bend the truth a little."

I felt a buzzing in my pocket. It was the prepaid cell phone. There was a message on it. I pressed play and listened to a deep, scratchy, stoner-type voice: "Dude...I don't know how to tell you this, but I hope you have insurance, 'cause a motherfucking muffin fell and crushed your Kia...I am not lying."

CRYING ON COMMAND

"**I CAN CRY ON COMMAND.**"

"You can what?" I asked.

"I can cry on command. It's one of the most effective selling tools that I've ever seen," Don Just told me over lunch at Pike's Soda Shop.

Don Just is the former CEO of The Martin Agency in Richmond. In his fifteen years at the helm, he helped grow Martin from fourteen employees to over three hundred. Don is one of the most earnest, sincere, genuine people I've ever met. He's also tough, no nonsense, serious, and a born leader. So hearing him say he can fake cry caused me to nearly choke on my pecan-crusted chicken.

"Seriously, you can cry on command?"

"I only use it when I really need it," he replied, and I could see in his eyes that he was not bullshitting me.

"So it's kind of like a superpower?" I asked.

"You might say that," he said with a proud smile. "A few years back we were pitching for the Virginia antismoking business. We were presenting to a room of ten members of their executive board. In fact, one of the people on the board was Peter Coughter." (Peter is a fellow professor with Don at VCU Brand Center in Richmond and a good friend of mine.) "We had shown our strategy and a couple of campaigns, and then I stood up to do the close.

"I told them that I had a whole closing prepared about how we are the best agency for your business, but 'I'm not going to go with what I had planned on saying,'" Don said, as he looked at me across the table. "'Right now,' I said to them, 'I'm thinking about Sarah. Sarah is a woman who works with us in our office. She has been a smoker her whole life. She's tried to quit many times. But she just can't do it. Sarah has two kids and she told me how badly she wants to quit because she's setting such a bad example for her children.'" Don then looked at me and said, "I paused for a second here, and summoned the tears. 'Sarah wants to be cigarette-free, but smoking has a grip on her. It controls her life.' I reached up and wiped the tears away and continued what I was saying. 'I want to win this business to help people like Sarah.'

"I paused and wiped my eyes again and looked around the room," Don said. "Everyone on the committee was misty-eyed. Everyone except for Coughter. He had his head in his hands."

"Why?" I asked.

"Oh, he had seen me do it before," Don said as he let out a laugh, which I was convinced was not fake.

"Did you win the pitch?"

"Of course we won. It's a gift. And it works every time."

I was fascinated by Don's ability. It was amazing.

I can't do much of anything on command. Well, except maybe fart on command, but that wouldn't win us many pitches.

I've told this story to a lot of people, and everyone has the same reaction: it's awesome, incredible, and pretty much unbelievable. Everyone I've shared the story with was impressed with Don's gift.

Everyone except for Ashley Reker, the digital director at BooneOakley.

"Oh, yeah, I do that all the time," Ashley said, when I told her about Don.

"You can cry on command?" I asked, skeptically.

"My ability to cry on command has gotten me out of seven speeding tickets," Ashley boasted.

"Are you serious?" I laughed.

"It's one of my talents," Ashley said.

My mouth fell open.

"It's not just the crying, Dave, it's the story-telling. From the moment that the blue lights come on until the officer is standing outside the window of my car is usually less than sixty seconds," Ashley explained. "So you have to think fast. You have to create a sad story. And more importantly, you have to believe that story. Usually, 'a guy did me wrong' type of story works best: my husband left me, my boyfriend cheated on me, my boyfriend broke up with me . . ."

I just stood there, listening in amazement.

"Once I pick my story, then my whole body must get involved. I act really flustered. If the officer asks for my license and registration, I act like I have no idea where it is, even though I know exactly where it is. I work myself into a state of being very upset. And then the tears flow."

"And they buy it?" I asked.

"It works every time."

"That is just unbelievable," I said to Ashley.

"It's true," she said proudly. "But, like I said before, you're creating a story: a real-life story the police officer is now a part of—and has a role in. Every story needs a villain (the boyfriend), a heroine (me), and a hero (the police officer). It's about finding the right story that, in letting you go without a ticket, the police officer gets to be the hero."

"Wow, that's genius," I said.

"It's just like how the Virginia antismoking client got to be the hero by awarding Don (the heroine) the business—and allowing him to beat the villain (smoking)."

I walked away from Ashley's office, laughing to myself. Ashley was seriously impressive. I had an idea, and turned around to go back to her office.

"How'd you like to be on our 'new business' team?"

"I would, but my boyfriend said he'd break up with me if I took on any more work."

Then she burst into tears.

PART TWO
HOW DID I GET HERE?

And you may ask yourself, how did I get here?
—Talking Heads

A FEW YEARS AGO, AMID THE NUTTINESS AND WONDERFULNESS OF THIS BUSINESS, I STOPPED TO REFLECT ON WHAT THE HELL I WAS DOING FOR A LIVING. I looked back on my childhood and realized that a career in advertising wasn't just thrust on me. I had been unconsciously preparing for it since I was a little kid.

CAMELS UNDER THE TREE

GROWING UP IN THE HEART OF TOBACCO ROAD IN NORTH CAROLINA, IT'S AMAZING THAT I NEVER SMOKED CIGARETTES. Everyone smoked cigarettes. My dad, Sid, smoked filterless Camels. My mom, Pat, smoked Parliaments. Aunt Hallie smoked Pall Malls. Uncle Pete smoked Winstons. Aunt Shirley smoked Tareytons. Uncle Sam puffed on Lucky Strikes. Everyone in the family smoked except Grandma Jenny. She was a bit more sophisticated; she dipped snuff. Tube Rose.

All those cigarettes made for some very smoky Christmas Eve get-togethers. At least it was always easy for grown-ups to know what to buy for one another. The adults in the family would simply draw names. So if my dad drew Sam, he knew that he could buy a carton of Lucky Strikes and Sam would be happy. Everyone wanted cigarettes for Christmas. It was the perfect gift.

The funny thing was, everyone hated walking to the counter at the Butner IGA to buy a different brand. They all smoked, but they all were very particular about what they smoked. And what they didn't smoke. I was learning something about brand loyalty and didn't even know it. Watching my dad, the Camel loyalist (or should I say addict?), buy a carton of Lucky Strikes was about as unusual as watching Dale Earnhardt Jr. hop in a Ford. Dad was a Camel man, and to him any other brand was clearly inferior. He would always apologize to the checkout guy for buying Lucky Strikes: "These are a present for a friend. I smoke Camels." Like the checkout guy really gave a shit.

We'd go home and I'd wrap the two cartons of cigs. Then we'd go to Grandma Jenny's house for Christmas Eve dinner and my sister Lisa and I would put the presents under the tree. We'd stack the brightly wrapped presents for Uncle Sam and Aunt Hallie right beside the other four presents that were shaped almost exactly the same: About fifteen inches long, four inches tall and two inches wide.

After having a wonderfully smoky meal of ham, turkey, biscuits, and dressing, we'd go into the den to open presents. One of the kids would have the honor of passing out the gifts. Usually it was Jodie, Sam and Shirley's daughter, because she was the oldest. "This one's for you, Mama." And she would hand one to Shirley, who opened the gift with great anticipation.

As soon as she started to tear the paper off, Aunt Shirley would exclaim, "Oh, someone knew just what I wanted!" Then she'd hold up the red-and-white carton of Tareytons for everyone to see.

"I bought those for you, Shirley," my mom would say.

"Thank you so much, Pat," Shirley would say. "That was really thoughtful." This fake surprise—and I guess, real joy—was repeated five more times as all the others opened their cancer sticks. This same scene unfolded every year.

But Lisa, my mischievous and oftentimes ingenious younger sister, had an idea on how to shake things up a bit one year. We'd simply change the nametags on the gifts. So instead of Sid getting a carton of Camels, he'd open Winstons. And so on. Lisa and I were quite pleased with our plan for Christmas Eve, 1977.

Aunt Hallie was the first to open her gift. The look on her face when she saw Parliaments was one of sheer disbelief. "I don't smoke these. This is the weak menthol stuff that Pat smokes."

At the same time Sid opened a pack of Winstons. "I don't smoke anything with filters. These cigarettes are made for women."

Uncle Pete quickly took offense and piped in, "Are you calling me a woman? You always thought you were better than me."

Uncle Sam opened his Camels and said, "These are what the guys in San Francisco suck on when they aren't sucking on other things."

Everyone was pissed off, except for Grandma Jenny. She sat in her rocking chair in the corner, grinned at Lisa, and knowingly said, "None of them needs to be smoking anyway." She then took a dip of her Tube Rose, winked, and said, "Hand me my spit cup."

I wish I'd done this ad.

A NASTY HABIT

GRANDMA JENNY WAS NOT A HIGHLY EDUCATED WOMAN. In fact, I'm not sure that she completed the eighth grade. But she had something that most diploma-toting folks didn't: she had a good turn about her. In her book, that was the highest compliment anyone could ever give.

According to Grandma Jenny, if someone had a good turn about them, they were good people. The kind of folks you'd like to sit down and have a beer with. But Grandma Jenny never drank, so I guess she would actually sit and have a glass of sweet tea with them. A person with a good turn about them would stop by and help you start your lawnmower, then hang out for a few minutes and shoot the bull with you.

Grandma Jenny wasn't a fan of preachers, lawyers, or anyone who put on highfalutin airs. She was about as real as real could get. I believed in Grandma Jenny. Probably more than I believed in Jesus. Often times, when I had to make a critical decision in my life I would think: *WWJD: What Would Jenny Do?*

One of these junctures in my life happened when I was fourteen. I was on the Hawley School eighth grade field trip. One Friday morning at five thirty, all 118 of us acne growers met in front of the school. We boarded three buses for a trip that no doubt would have made Senator Jesse Helms burst with pride. We were going to support the agriculture of our state. We were leaving Creedmoor and heading down Tobacco Road to Winston-Salem. And what pray tell, lay waiting at the end of

Tobacco Road? Why the R. J. Reynolds cigarette factory, of course: the perfect place to educate young adults about the benefits of tobacco.

I guess they figured that we weren't just kids anymore. We were *consumers*. I don't think my parents had to sign permission slips or anything like that to give me the OK to go. I remember telling them where we were going and my dad said, "That's where they make Camels. Keep a close eye on that process. You'll see that they use better tobacco than they do to make the Winstons. It's more golden colored. That's quality. You're a lucky kid, David, to go on field trip like this."

He was wrong about that. The lucky kids were the kids from Tennessee, who I imagined got to go to the Jack Daniels factory, or the eighth graders in Missouri who got to go to St. Louis to see how Budweiser was made.

After about a two-hour drive we made it to our destination. The factory itself was actually kind of cool. I had never seen so many cigarettes in my life. They were making millions of Salems. We saw how the tobacco was chopped to just the right thickness and rolled by those giant machines. We saw how they were separated into groups of twenty, and put neatly into Salem packs and then smartly wrapped in protective plastic to keep the rich flavor in.

At the end of the assembly line, our tour guide, a nice looking woman in her mid-twenties, asked the question we had all been waiting for: "Does anyone want some samples? We have Camels, Winstons, and Salems. One pack per person. Oh yeah, and for those of you who don't smoke, we have fresh Levi Garrett chewing tobacco."

That moment was a WWJD moment. Not *What Would Jesus Do?* but *What Would Jenny Do?* I knew in an instant that Grandma Jenny wouldn't take the cigarettes. "I'll take a pouch of Levi, please," came out of my mouth, like I had been saying it for years. And with those words, I started my love affair with Levi.

That weekend when I got back to Creedmoor, I rode my bike over to Grandma Jenny's house. I walked into her kitchen with a spit cup and a big chaw of Levi crammed into my cheek. She looked up from the puzzle she was putting together and gave me a funny look.

"Are you chewing tobacco?" she asked.

"Yes." I responded with glistening brown tobacco drool on my chin.

"Well, I'm glad you haven't taken up smoking. That is a nasty habit." she grinned at me and said, "Now come over here and hug my neck."

I CHEWED LEVI GARRETT CHEWING TOBACCO FOR THE NEXT 10 YEARS. I LOVED IT. HOW DID I STOP, YOU ASK? I WAS DRIVING TO SNOWSHOE, WEST VIRGINIA, TO GO SKIING. I WAS CHEWING LEVI AND SPITTING INTO A MCDONALD'S CUP THAT I KEPT BETWEEN MY LEGS IN THE DRIVER'S SEAT. (MY '77 CELICA DIDN'T HAVE CUP HOLDERS.)

AFTER SEVERAL HOURS OF HOLDING TOBACCO SPIT, THE MCDONALD'S CUP RUPTURED AND WARM TOBACCO SPIT ENGULFED MY TESTICLES. I QUICKLY STOPPED THE CAR, JUMPED OUT INTO THE EIGHTEEN-DEGREE WEATHER, AND STRIPPED OFF MY JEANS AND SPIT-SOAKED TIGHTIE-WHITIES, WHICH WERE NOT WHITE ANYMORE.

IT WAS AT THAT MOMENT I REALIZED THAT GRANDMA JENNY WAS WRONG. CHEWING TOBACCO WAS ALSO A NASTY HABIT. I HAVEN'T CHEWED SINCE.

COLD BEER

GREW UP IN CREEDMOOR, NORTH CAROLINA, A SMALL TOWN IN THE BIBLE BELT. You might say it was the buckle of the Bible Belt. There was a guy in town named Jess Sansings, who ran a thrift store. Jess drove a reconditioned silver U-Haul transfer truck around town collecting things at yard sales and flea markets to sell in his thrift shop.

One Saturday night after a few beers at the Butner Pool Hall, Jess had an idea to drum up some business. He grabbed a twelve-pack to go and drove over to see his buddy Tillman Hobgood at the Butner Sign Shop. He asked Tillman to paint a slogan on the side of his truck. The two of them drank and painted into the night.

On Sunday morning after Sunday school had started, Jess parked his truck across the street from the Creedmoor First Baptist Church. When the preaching was over, the congregation walked out of the church and saw Granville County's first mobile billboard. On the side of Jess' silver truck, three-foot-tall red letters screamed JESS SAVES.

It was my introduction to a big advertising idea.

But it wasn't until the spring of 1979 that I understood the incredible persuasive power of a big advertising idea. The student council elections at South Granville High were coming up, and I decided to throw my hat into the ring. I had never run for student council before, so I figured I'd better do something that made the other kids remember my name.

I devised my first advertising campaign. It was quite cutting edge for Creedmoor. Instead of the standard construction paper buttons that most candidates made with catchy slogans like *Vote for Pam*, I took it up a notch. My campaign used clever rhymes. Like, *Dave's my Fave*, and *I Rave about Dave*. Ingenious, huh? I didn't make my campaign buttons round. I made them in the shape of clip-on neckties. *Wave if you're voting 4 Dave*. In my mind, I was using techniques to get elected that no one had ever seen or thought of before.

I even resorted to bribery. On every campaign button I passed out, I stapled a piece of Dubble Bubble gum. Now this was true innovation. Not only was bubble gum a nice little treat, it was also banned at South Granville High. Which made me seem even cooler. I was the rebel who was willing to break the rules, and that's the type of guy the kids wanted on student council. At least that's what Bobbie Wooten told me. "You're a shoo-in, Dave," she said.

I wanted to win, and win in a landslide. So on every break between classes, before school, after school, and at lunch, I worked the crowds. I gave out gum and asked the other kids to vote for me. I campaigned hard.

Not that I really needed to. I was running against Tom Young. He didn't appear to be much competition. He lived in the northern part of the county and this was his first year at South Granville. He didn't know many people, and people sure didn't know him. On top of that, he was kind of a skinny nerd and skinny nerds don't often do well in the popularity contests that are student council elections. I was going to win and win big.

Before lunch on election day, everyone in the eleventh grade seemed to be wearing my necktie buttons. I don't even think Tom had buttons. If he did, no one was wearing them. Voting was scheduled to take place in fifth period, the first class after lunch. As I walked toward the cafeteria to get a plate of chili con carne, I was feeling pretty good about things. I was feeling even better when Cecilia Wilson, the hottest girl at SG, pinned a *Dave's my Fave* tie right below her incomparable cleavage. If my day had ended right there, it would have been perfect.

But it didn't end there. I walked into the cafeteria and there it was, hanging above the door at the end of the slow-moving line of students heading to pick up their lunch trays: the "October Surprise" of this election.

It was a hand-drawn sign on poster board. From across the cafeteria, you could see what it said in large block letters: COLD BEER. As I waited in line, I said to Willis Herman, who was beside me, "That's funny as hell. How long do you think it will be before Carl T. Weaver takes it down?" Carl T. Weaver was the principal at South Granville and there was no doubt that he would not be amused by a poster advertising that beer was served at his high school.

"Carl T. will take it down as soon as he sees it. I just hope I get a Budweiser to go with my chili before he does," Willis said with a chuckle.

"I hope they have Schlitz," said Billy Tillman. "I'm a Schlitz man… if you know what I mean." This was hilarious. Every kid in line was talking about how they were going to drink beer for lunch. Without a doubt, this was the best prank since the seniors soaped the fountain last spring.

As the line to get food moved closer, I could see that there was some really small type on the bottom of the poster. I couldn't read it until I was right under it. When I read it, I knew that I'd been beat. It said: *COLD BEER is not served here. But now that I've got your attention, vote for Tom Young!*

Wow. Tom wasn't a nerd. He was a genius. If I hadn't been running, I would have voted for him. But I voted for myself. Mainly to avert the shutout.

It was a huge lesson in advertising and one that I've never forgotten: A big idea always beats a big execution. And beer always beats bubble gum.

Even though I lost the election, I trace my love of ice-cold Budweiser back to this poster.

THE WEATHER PICTURE

MY FRIENDSHIP WITH PAULA PEARCE STARTED IN THE FIFTH GRADE. It was 1972, and we were in Mrs. Curl's class at Hawley Middle School. On election day, Mrs. Curl had all of her students vote for the next president. It was a secret ballot. After we voted, she tallied the votes. It was a landslide: 29 votes for Nixon, 2 votes for McGovern. Paula Pearce and I were the only ones in our class who voted for McGovern. Paula and I didn't fall for Tricky Dick.

As the years passed, we became very good friends. By the time we were in tenth grade, Dick had become quite the topic of conversation between us. As in who had one and who didn't.

I think Paula changed my gender first, but I'm not sure. All I know is that at some point she started calling me Davida and I started calling her Paul. Then she started calling my best friends Billy and Mark "Willamena" and "Marquita." We didn't change anyone else's name. There was only one Paul.

Paula was a tall African-American girl. She had a big puffy afro, a wide nose, and the most beautiful mocha skin. I guess you would say she was big-boned. She wasn't fat, but she didn't have a runway model figure either. If you put shoulder pads on her, I have no doubt that she could have started for our football team. She could pass for a boy. And there was no doubt that she thought my friends and I could pass for girls.

One day at school, Billy, Mark, and I were sitting in the cafeteria not eating our school lunch. Paula walked up to our table.

"What's up, Paul?" I asked.

"Hey, Paul," Billy said.

"Hello ladies," Paula responded. "I found something that one of you girls dropped." And she pulled a tampon from her pocket and tossed it onto our table. We scattered like she had tossed a live hand grenade.

"Oh, you girls haven't gotten your period yet? You girls are soooo sensitive."

Mostly our exchanges were nothing more than "Hello, Davida," and "Hello, Paul," but Paula usually got the better of me. She was in all of my classes so she had ample opportunity. One of her better efforts occurred in French class. Our teacher, Mrs. Woodlief, would walk around the class asking us questions in French, and of course we were supposed to answer in French.

"*Comment allez-vous?*" she asked me.

"*Ça va,*" I answered.

She looked over at Rick Tate, a chubby kid who had his head down on his desk and was falling asleep.

"*Rick, es tu fatigué?*" Mrs. Woodlief asked.

Rick looked up, bleary eyed and said, "What?"

"*En francais, Rick. Es tu fatigué?*"

Rick just stared at her. Mrs. Woodlief grew impatient and said it louder.

"*Es tu fatigué? Rick, es tu fatigué?*"

"I am not…" Rick started to answer.

"*En francais,*" Mrs. Woodlief interrupted again.

Rick slammed his French book shut and blurted out, "I am not fat and gay, you bitch." He got up and walked out of the classroom with Mrs. Woodlief close behind. We sat there in stunned disbelief. We had never heard anyone call a teacher a bitch before. At least not to her face.

Paula broke the silence and said out loud, *"Rick est fatigué. Et Davida est skinny et gay."* The whole class cracked up. Over the next few weeks, *Rick est fatigué and Davida est skinny et gay* became South Granville High's new catchphrase. It was more popular than *Where's the beef?* Everyone was saying it. I must admit that it was very funny. But it was killing me that Paula had gotten the upper hand in our "You're a girl, you're a boy" game.

I needed to one-up her. I racked my brain for weeks, when every night the answer was right in front of me. Every night, the Oakley family watched *Action News 5* on WRAL from Raleigh. And we weren't alone. It was the highest rated news show in the Triangle. Not that there were a lot of choices. There were only four TV channels at the time.

The reason *Action News 5* consistently beat WTVD's *Eyewitness News* wasn't just because they had Charlie Gaddy and Bobbi Batista. (Although Bobbi Batista was very easy on the eyes and went on to become CNN's first anchorwoman.) It was because they had "The Biggest Name in Weather": Bob DeBardelaben. Bob was a gregarious, balding man in his mid-fifties. He did the weather with a homey, personal touch. We loved it when he would say things like, *"Tonight's low in Raleigh will be 39, in Durham 38, and in Creedmoor it will dip down to 37."* Having your town mentioned in the same breath with the big cities of Raleigh and Durham? Really cool.

Bob also did a segment right after the 5-Day Forecast where he featured a "Weather Picture" that a young local artist had made. These were mostly crude crayon drawings done by first or second graders, showing things like a flower in the rain with a caption like: "April Showers bring May Flowers." And Bob would always say something nice about the picture: *"Tonight's Weather Picture is from Emily Haney. She's in the first grade at Millbrook Elementary here in Raleigh. I sure hope Emily's right that this rain will bring us some flowers. Nice job, Emily."*

That evening, right as Bob was introducing Tom Suiter with sports, it came to me. I asked my mom if we still had any crayons. She said that Lisa had some. So I borrowed my sister's Crayolas and went to work. I started drawing a weather picture in the style of a second grader. I drew a big yellow sun in the upper right-hand corner of the page. I drew a little boy standing with his dog in front of his house, waving with a comic strip bubble above his head that said, "I love you Bob D!" With his other hand the boy was pointing up in the sky at an airplane flying overhead. And then I signed it really big in the lower right hand corner. Paul Pearce. Age 7. Butner, NC.

Sending in a weather picture signed Paul Pearce was a pretty good idea. But there was no telling if and when Bob would ever show it. He might have hundreds of other pictures in line to show. It might not get shown for years. Then I had a brainstorm that turned a pretty good idea into a brilliant one. Paula's birthday was less than two weeks away. And I made one last addition to my weather picture. I added a banner behind the airplane that said "Happy Birthday to Me. Feb 23." I got an envelope and mailed it to WRAL the next morning.

At school the next day, I saw Paula in Mrs. Criddlebaugh's homeroom. "How's your home economics class going, Davida?" she asked.

I ignored her question and said, "Paul, all I have to say is watch *Action News 5* next week. They are doing an exposé that will offer proof to the world that you are a boy."

Paula laughed and said, "Girl, you're crazy."

"I'm not crazy. I'm serious. They are running it next Tuesday, the twenty-third."

"The twenty-third is my birthday. I hope you've been shopping for my present," Paula replied.

"You'll get your present on *Action News 5*."

The next week and a half went by slower than any week and a

half in history. I told everyone who would listen to watch the news on February 23. I was obsessed with it.

Yet I had no real reason to believe that Bob DeBardelaben would actually show Paul's drawing. I started to get a little nervous as the day approached. What if I had run my mouth to all of these people and he didn't show it? *I'll be a joke,* I worried. But I guessed no more of a joke than being a boy named Davida.

At long last, the twenty-third arrived. In social studies class that morning, we were discussing current events and I raised my hand to ask a question. Coach Hawkins called on me.

"Please watch *Action News 5* tonight. Bob DeBardelaben is breaking a story that Paul Pearce is truly a boy," I said.

Coach Hawkins, who hated me, said, "Mr. Oakley, first of all, Bob DeBardelaben is the weather man and he doesn't do reporting, and second, if I watch and there is nothing on there tonight, you will have a week of detention with me." The hatred from Coach Hawkins was not unrequited. I despised him so much from football practice that I fantasized about the kind of tortures he could suffer (none of which could be included in this family publication).

When the bell rang at three fifteen, I walked through the halls and repeated, "Watch Bob DeBardelaben tonight, watch Bob DeBardelaben tonight," to everyone I passed. On the bus ride home, I even told Ricky Carpenter to watch it. And his family didn't even own a TV.

I found a spot on our couch at five o'clock and sat through two reruns of *The Andy Griffith Show.* Both episodes had Warren as the deputy. Even if I hadn't been waiting for the Weather Picture, they would have seemed like they were three hours long. Each.

When the clock that I was watching changed from 5:59 to 6:00, I heard that familiar voice. *"Covering the Carolinas from Manteo to Murphy, it's Action News 5. With Charlie Gaddy, Bobbi Batista, Tom Suiter with sports, and the biggest name in weather, Bob DeBardelaben."*

Charlie opened with a story about a house fire in Franklinton and then Bobbi told us about a Kwik Pik in Fuquay-Varina being robbed.

Finally around 6:18, it was time for the weather. Bob went through the morning lows and the afternoon highs and talked about a cold front that was sweeping in from the Canadian Rockies. By the time he gave the 5-Day Forecast, I was so geeked with anticipation that I was on the verge of throwing up. And then Bob said, "Tonight we have a very special weather picture. Actually, it's a birthday picture."

As soon as I heard those words, I knew it was happening. "It's from Paul Pearce from Butner." The camera cut away from Bob and my drawing came up full screen. I wanted to scream, but I didn't dare because I didn't want to miss a syllable. Bob continued gushing about the picture. "It says 'Happy Birthday to me.' Just a beautiful picture. Paul is quite the artist."

And then Bobbi Batista joined in, "It looks like Paul has a crush on you, Bob. What does it say there? I love you Bob D?"

Bob said, "Yes it does and I'm a big fan of his, too. Happy Birthday, Paul."

Our phone rang immediately. It was Willamena. He was laughing so hard he could barely talk. I got him off the phone and it rang again. This time it was Paula.

"Hello," I said.

"David, I'm going to kill you," she said.

"Did you just call me David?" I asked through my laughter.

"Yes," she said.

And she hung up.

She never called me Davida again.

At least not in high school. But the first word I heard when I walked into our twentieth high school reunion was "Davida." Which was quickly followed by Paula exclaiming, "You're still the prettiest girl at South Granville."

Paula Pearce and me together as seniors in high school.

THE HUSTLER

TOM WASHINGTON SHOULD HAVE BEEN SUSPICIOUS.
It was mid-August. And the temperature was close to a hundred degrees. It must have seemed at least a little bit unusual to see a fourteen-year-old riding his bike to the Butner Kwik Pik wearing jeans.

While all the other kids were wearing shorts, I was sweating my ass off. Yes, my Levi's were hot. But not as hot as what was up my sleeve…or about to be up my pant leg.

That summer, I was working. I had a job. I was self-employed.

My first foray into entrepreneurship was a relatively inexpensive business to start. All I needed was a bike. And a couple of pieces of equipment: two rubber bands. I wore one around each ankle.

Every day, I'd park my bike by the *Butner-Creedmoor News* paper box in front of the Kwik Pik. I'd walk inside, casually stroll over to the magazine rack and start thumbing through a *Mad* magazine or a *Boys' Life*. As soon as Tom Washington, the store manager, turned his head, I'd reach up to the top shelf and grab a *Playboy*. Quickly, I'd stuff it up my pant leg and stretch the rubber band around the magazine to hold it in place around my ankle. Then I'd look at the round mirror in the corner of the store to make sure Tom still wasn't looking. If he wasn't, I'd grab a *Penthouse* and stuff it up the other pant leg.

Then I'd stand up, grab a pack of Juicy Fruit and go pay. I'd walk out of the store, hop on my Schwinn, and ride home with my booty.

At first this was just a hobby. Just a little something for my personal enjoyment. But soon I realized that maybe I could make a little money with this. I could sell these things at school.

My first sale was on the first day of school in the eighth grade. It was a *Penthouse* that had a "Pet of the Month" centerfold who looked a lot like our sixth grade English teacher, Mrs. Strand. I sold it to Billy Tillman for $5. When you consider my 10-cent investment in Juicy Fruit, my profit margin was a whopping 5000 percent. Not a bad business model. I was selling five or six magazines a week that fall. I was making major cash.

By the end of August, I had "collected" over 60 magazines. They weren't all *Playboys* and *Penthouses* either. I had *Club*, *Club International*, *Stag*, and *Oui*, which I called O.U.I. At the time, I had no idea that *oui* was the French word for *yes*.

And of course, there was *Hustler*. *Hustler* was a little more, how can I say this, *graphic* than the others.

Every fourteen-year-old boy knew that you could see naked breasts in *Playboy*. You could see naked breasts and pubic hair in *Penthouse*. But *Hustler* was the first to show a vagina. (Or as we boys affectionately called it, the pink taco.) This alone put *Hustler* in high demand.

But nothing compared to the frenzy the August 1977 issue of *Hustler* created. It was the first magazine to use scratch-'n'-sniff technology. Where did Larry Flynt employ this technology? On the centerfold, of course.

Not many seventh graders that I knew had ever seen a vagina. Much less ever smelled one. I knew that this magazine was going to be in very, very high demand. So I added it to my collection.

For the record, when you scratched that centerfold, it gave off the distinctive scent of cotton candy. To this day, whenever I go the state fair or the circus and smell cotton candy, I immediately think of Miss

August reclining buck-naked, spread eagle on a black couch.

I told my buddies at Hawley Middle School that I had a copy of the scratch-'n'-sniff *Hustler*. And that I was willing to sell it. Two hours later, Dale Elliott and Larry Howard walked up to me in the school cafeteria. I had a taker.

Dale said, "Larry wants to buy the *Hustler*."

"What are you, his spokesman?" I replied.

"You know Larry. He's kind of shy."

I looked at Larry and said, "You gonna buy it?" He nodded yes. "It's $20, ya know."

"That's a lot of money," he complained.

"It's a *Hustler*. It's scratch-'n'-sniff. You not only see it, you smell it."

Larry agreed to give me $20 the next morning.

I went home after school and went to work. This time, I wasn't adding to my collection. I needed to doctor the price printed on the cover of the *Hustler*. I used an X-Acto knife and carefully cut the $2.25 price tag off the cover. Even though I didn't actually buy the magazine, the mark-up to $20 might seem a little excessive. Either way, to a fourteen-year-old, its contents were priceless.

The next morning, Larry and Dale were waiting for me when I got off the school bus.

"Do you have the *Hustler*? Do you have the *Hustler*?" Larry asked impatiently.

"Yeah, shut up, I've got it. Have you got the money?"

Larry reached into his pocket and pulled out a $20 bill. He handed it to me. I handed him the Hustler, neatly packaged in a brown paper bag.

"I can't hold this all day. I'll get in trouble," Larry fretted.

"Put it in your locker and get it at the end of the day," I said.

"No, I might get caught."

Dale chimed in, "If you're so worried about it, give it to me. I'll keep it in my locker and I'll give it back to you at the end of the day. How about that?"

Larry nodded his head and handed the bag to Dale.

"Enjoyed doing business with you fellas," I said as I walked to Mrs. Park's science class, grinning at the thought of what I could buy for $20.

The next morning I got off the school bus the same way I always did. And like the day before, a Howard was waiting for me. But this time it was Harry Howard. Larry's older brother. He was older by about 5 minutes. They were twins, but Harry had all the smarts. He also had a speech impediment. One that made any attempt at intimidation useless. Every R he spoke sounded like a W.

As soon as I stepped off the bus and my Converse All-Stars hit the gravel, Harry was in my face saying, "You took advantage of my bwothah. You took advantage of my bwothah."

"What are you talking about?" I said I as I kept walking toward the front door of Hawley Middle School.

"You sold Lawwy that magazine. You wipped him off."

"What do you mean I ripped him off? It was worth every penny."

"You wipped him off."

"That was a *Hustler*. It was the scratch-'n'-sniff issue." I immediately thought Harry thought I had overcharged Larry, so to accentuate the rarity of the magazine I said, "My dad bought it at an adult book store."

"I don't cawe whewe you got it! It didn't have any pictuwes in it! All the pictuwes wewe gone!"

When he said this, I stopped dead in my tracks. "What?" I said.

"Thewe wewe no pictuwes in it. When he got home, thewe was nothing but stowies in it. And cawtoons. No naked giwls."

"Well, when I sold it to him, it had all the pictures in it."

"Not anymowe."

"Larry was so scared when I sold it to him that he gave it to Dale Elliott to keep in his locker until the end of the day. Maybe you should talk with Dale…"

"You sold it to him."

"All sales are final."

As I walked into the school building, I had a new appreciation for Dale Elliott. That guy was going to have a bright future. Clearly, he was a genius.

I also started thinking about Larry and how disappointed he must have been. All worked up, all day long yesterday, counting the minutes until the end of seventh period history class, thinking he was going to see—and smell—some naked girls. He probably sprinted off the school bus, clutching the brown paper bag, ran straight to his bedroom, and locked the door behind him. Dropped his pants and opened the magazine. No pictures. No skin. No scratch-'n'-sniff.

The thought of Larry with his pants at his ankles, frantically looking for one, just one picture, brought a smile to my face. I chuckled to myself as I walked down the hallway. "That has to be the most embarrassing thing ever. What a dumbass."

"Hi, Mr. Oakley," said Mrs. Strand, who was a vision of attractiveness as she stood by the door to her classroom full of sixth graders.

"Hello, Mrs. Strand," I said with a grin.

"Could you come here for a second?" Mrs. Strand motioned with her finger for me to follow her.

She turned and walked into her classroom. I followed her. She stopped behind her desk and opened the drawer. Inside, on top of some files, I saw a *Penthouse* magazine. It had rubber band marks across the cover.

"So…you think she looks like me?"

I felt a flush come over me as my face transformed to match the shade of Mrs. Strand's ruby red lipstick. From the corner of my eye,

I saw Larry Howard sitting in the front row, with a satisfied look on his face. My shoulders slumped, and I knew that my days as a *Hustler* hustler had come to an end.

GRASSHOPPER CASSEROLE

I HAVE A PIECE OF KERRY GONZALEZ'S POTTERY IN MY OFFICE. It's a beautiful, raku-glazed, covered jar. I keep it as a memento of the friendship we had when I was a teenager, and as a reminder of a lesson that he taught me back then—a lesson that has really helped me in my advertising career.

Kerry Gonzalez started working at Cedar Creek Pottery, our family business, when I was fifteen. He was probably about ten years older than me, which when you're fifteen is a lifetime. He was a potter who specialized in raku glazing. (Raku is a firing technique that causes random cracking in the glaze.) I knew a lot about pottery, since my parents were potters. They both worked in stoneware and porcelain. But Kerry's pottery was something completely different.

He had a car. Actually it was a van. A red-and-white VW van: the mid-'70s' hippie status symbol of choice. He had a nice house that he rented at Cedar Creek with a killer record collection and an even better Pioneer sound system. He had so many Emmylou Harris albums that I thought that he actually knew her. He was also a big fan of Bob Wills and the Texas Playboys. I really wasn't that into their music, but I figured that they must be cool if they were known as playboys. Kerry had a great sense of humor and I really looked up to him. You might say he was my idol for a while. I guess he enjoyed my company as well, because he was always asking me to help him whenever his monthly shipment of clay was delivered. Boxes of clay were fifty pounds each, and we were too cheap or poor to invest in a dolly to move them from the parking lot to his studio. I guess the reasoning was: why spend money on a dolly when Davy would do it for free?

One of the many things that set Kerry apart from the other potters was that his studio was pristine. His tools were hung in an orderly way on the wall beside his wheel. He swept his studio at least three times a day. My father Sid's studio, on the other hand, was never clean. Every couple of years, when the pile of empty clay boxes, broken bisque-fired pots and glaze buckets made it too cluttered to walk through, Sid just built another studio. But I digress.

Back to Kerry, the organized one. One day he was getting ready for a big show. Not the typical show where potters packed up their wares and drove to Blacksburg or Virginia Beach to sit on a folding chair all weekend to try to sell their stuff. The show Kerry was preparing for was kind of an open house. He called it his "Open Studio" show. He had invited about twenty-five of his friends to come over and see all of his new work. Kerry was meticulously cleaning his studio again, and placing his latest creations on displays for his friends to go gaga over. I was just hanging out and listening to him tell me how awesome the new glazes were on his casserole dishes, and how his friends were going to be blown away by his creative genius. Kerry was just joking around. Or at least I think he was. Anyway, his friends were coming over around seven o'clock, so at six, he left his studio and went up to his house to get showered and ready to entertain.

I wasn't invited to the soiree, so I headed down to our house. About halfway home, a grasshopper jumped up and landed on my shirt. This wasn't out of the ordinary; grasshoppers were more common than thunderstorms in the North Carolina summer. I grabbed the grasshopper from my chest and before I smashed him, I had an idea.

Five minutes later, I had captured about twenty nice-size grasshoppers. I took them up to Kerry's studio and put them all in one of his precious new casserole dishes. *This is hilarious*, I thought. *When his friends pick up the top to admire his lovely casserole, my little grasshoppers will jump out all over his studio.* I must say, I was pretty impressed with my own genius. I closed the door to his studio, and headed back down to our house for a second time.

On the way, Woofer and Tweeter, our two crazy Irish setter puppies, ran up to greet me. I petted each of them and then continued walking. Then I saw a fresh pile of puppy shit right in the middle of our brick walkway. Damn puppies. I went to the toolshed to get a small shovel to scoop it off the walk before someone stepped in it. Then another idea popped into my head. Puppy shit would make a nice casserole surprise. I LOLed. (I actually laughed out loud because LOLing wasn't really invented yet.)

I took the fresh, steaming pile to Kerry's studio and placed it into a second casserole. Boy, were his guests in for a big surprise tonight. I didn't stop laughing to myself for the next fifteen hours. I think I even sleep-laughed, if that's possible.

The laughing stopped at exactly 6:47 the next morning. "Did you put dog shit in Kerry's studio?" yelled my dad, as he shook me to wake me up.

"What?" I asked.

"Kerry said that you put shit in his pottery. I've never seen anyone as mad as Kerry in all of my life. Now get out of bed and get up there and wash all of his pots. And I mean *scrub* them. And when you're done with that, you get your ass up to his house and apologize to him."

So I got out of bed and headed up to Kerry's studio. It was pretty much as I'd left it, except for an empty bottle of wine and a couple of wine glasses on the tables. I lifted the top of the casserole that I'd put the grasshoppers in. There were several grasshoppers still inside. I took them outside and set them free. Then I went back inside and opened the casserole that contained the dog shit. There was nothing inside except for a brown stain and that unmistakable stench. I scrubbed both of the casseroles with Joy—the dishwashing liquid, not happiness. I dried them off and returned them to their treasured places on Kerry's display.

Just as I put the casserole down, I heard the side door open. It was Kerry. Before I could get one word of apology out of my mouth, he yelled, "How dare you desecrate my work? How dare you desecrate my work?"

Sensing an opportunity to use my teenage wit I replied, "I didn't desecrate it, I defecated it."

"You think that's funny? You think it's funny that you ruined my open house?" Suddenly I was really afraid that he was going to jump over his potter's wheel and beat the dog shit out of me.

"I'm really sorry that I ruined your party, Kerry. I really am."

"You should be," he replied. "It killed the whole night."

"C'mon," I said, "Don't your friends have a sense of humor?"

"Of course they do. The grasshoppers were funny. I even laughed at that. I even told them that the grasshoppers were the work of Sid's pizza-faced son. The grasshoppers were funny. What wasn't funny was when Carol Montague opened the green casserole and screamed, 'Oh my God, gross!' In a split second, this entire studio was engulfed in a noxious cloud of dog shit stench. Everyone ran outside to escape the odor. And the party was over," Kerry said.

I could tell he was hurt. Maybe some of his friends had made fun of him. Clearly he was extremely embarrassed by my practical joke.

"I'm really sorry, Kerry," I told him and I meant it. He accepted my apology and handed me a broom.

"How about sweeping over there? I think I see a little clay dust on the floor."

I've thought about this incident many times in the last thirty years or so. Every time, it brings a small grin to my face. I still think it's funny. But I learned a valuable lesson about humor that day.

It feels really good to make someone laugh. It's a rush. It's a high. It feels so good that the temptation is to follow it up with another witty line is often irresistible. But invariably, the second joke is never as good as the first one.

Humor is a wonderful and dangerous thing. And I'm certainly not an expert on humor. But I do know that you have to know where to draw the line.

So I keep one of Kerry's casseroles in my office to always remind me that one joke is enough. Whether it's in a TV spot, a banner ad, or at a client meeting. If you have a simple concept and you keep adding things, it can quickly turn a great idea into a pile of shit.

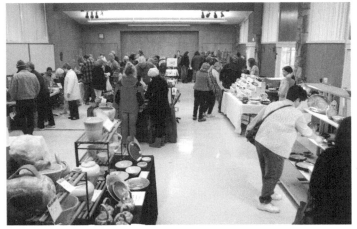

There's nothing more exciting for a kid than spending a weekend at a craft show.

OUT OF ORDER

Y OU RARELY SEE KIDS AT AN ARTS AND CRAFTS SHOW. That's because kids have a natural aversion to walking at 1 mph and looking at macramé, decoupage, and handmade dulcimers. Oh sure, you see infants in those backpack things and toddlers in strollers. But they're strapped down and have no choice.

As soon as kids outgrow their strollers, the smart ones at least will run up to a potter's exhibit and knock a vase or a bowl off the shelf. The crash of shattered porcelain or stoneware is invariably followed by a parent screaming, "This is the last crafts show I'm ever bringing you to!" And the kid smiles, the way Brer Rabbit did when Brer Fox threw him into the briar patch.

I spent a lot of time at craft shows when I was a kid. I didn't have an option. I'm a son of two potters.

Every year when I was growing up, the Oakleys took a trip to Virginia to do the Blacksburg Fall Crafts Fair. It was held at the Squires Student Center on the Virginia Tech campus. At the entrance to the exhibit hall there was a sign that read: *No one between the ages of 4 and 17 admitted. (Unless you are an indentured servant or the son or daughter of a craftsman. Or both. In which case you are not to leave the premises for the next 3 days.)*

Going to Blacksburg was a family trip, but certainly was not what one would call "a proper vacation." It was really a business trip, a chance for my parents, Sid and Pat, to sell their new pottery bowls, pitchers, and vases to a different audience. But for my sister Lisa and me, it doubled as a vacation. A break of sorts from loading and unloading the kilns, glazing pots, and scraping kiln shelves. Which is what we did pretty much nonstop for the week leading up to the craft show.

When we first got to a show, Lisa and I had another job to do: unload the shelves, the display cubes, and all of the boxes of pottery from our '73 Ford Econoline van. Next we set up our display, unwrapped all of the pottery and arranged it on the shelves. That usually took about two hours. Then came the hard part: for the next three days, we would wait on customers. Not waiting like a waiter waits on tables. Just waiting. We sat there, waiting for someone to buy a piece of pottery. There were a lot of lookers. People who would walk by and just look. Sometimes they would pick up a honey pot or a coffee mug and look at it closely. "Buy it, you'll like it," I would say under my breath to them, mimicking the old *Try it, you'll like it* Alka-Seltzer commercials. Lisa and I played a lot of tic-tac-toe and counted yawns. We passed the time as best we could.

On one particularly uneventful afternoon, I was so bored I could barely stay awake.

"Maybe a Coke will perk you up," my mom suggested. "Here's thirty cents. Go buy you one."

"Thanks, Mom," I said, thinking I'd much rather go over to the Hokie House and have a chilly beer. But I was fourteen and I didn't get served at the Hokie House until the next year. I took the change and walked out of our booth in search of a Coke machine. I found one in the foyer at the side entrance of Squires Hall. I dropped the quarter and nickel in without noticing the Out of Order sign. My money fell right into the change slot. I grabbed the coins and returned to our booth, now not only bored, but totally bummed. I sat down, slouched in the folding chair, and stared at a shelf of stoneware bowls.

But on that shelf, beside a half-empty cup of my dad's Nescafé, I spied something extraordinary. It was a roll of duct tape. Immediately, I had an idea. The boredom vanished. Suddenly, I was up to no good. And when you're up to no good, you always need an accomplice. So I asked Lisa to take a little walk with me.

We went back to the Coke machine. The foyer was full of people but as soon as it emptied out, I had a job to do. And so did Lisa. She was going to be the lookout. Her job was to let me know if anyone was coming into the room. My job was to make the Coke machine my own little personal ATM. The plan was simple: While Lisa stood guard, I stuffed duct tape up inside the change slot in the Coke machine. Then I removed the Out of Order sign.

The rest of the afternoon flew by. We helped a few customers at our parents' booth, but mostly we walked back and forth to the watch the action at the Coke machine. We saw four people kick the machine and two guys punch it. We also found out that this Coke machine had a lot of different nicknames. "SOB," "Douchebag," and "Fucker" were the most memorable.

By the end of the afternoon, I was starting to feel sorry for the poor machine. But not that sorry, because we could hardly wait to see what kind of loot awaited us. Once again, we waited for the room to clear and Lisa stood guard. I crouched down and reached up the coin return slot and pulled out the duct tape. Coins gushed out like it was a hot Vegas slot machine. Money was bouncing everywhere. Lisa had to leave her post as lookout to help scoop it up. We were stuffing our pockets as fast as possible, all the while praying that no one would open the door. Just as I picked up the last quarter a lady pushing a kid in a stroller walked in. She reached into her purse to get some change and looked at the Coke machine.

"I think it's out of order," I said.

She looked at me and said, "Thank you so much. You're such a nice boy."

I looked at the poor kid strapped in the stroller, grinned at Lisa and then got the hell out of there. We went back inside and counted our jackpot. It came to $23.75. This was more than my parents made selling pottery that day.

Looking back, I've often wondered if this incident didn't foreshadow a life of crime for me. Well, I did go into advertising.

T-SHIRT ENVY

FROM MY FIRST WEEK AS A FRESHMAN AT UNC, I WANTED TO BE AN INTRAMURAL CHAMPION. Not because I craved the glory of winning a sports championship. Not at all. I just wanted a Carolina IM Champion T-shirt. And I spent the next four years trying to get one.

I didn't even understand the shirt at first. It was a nice color of blue, but it wasn't Carolina blue. It was more like the color of a bluebird. In the middle of the shirt was a white foot with a black spot on the heel. I understood that part: Tar Heel. The type is what threw me. It read "Carolina IM Champion." I thought it was a misprint. They had obviously left out the apostrophe between the *I* and the *M*. "Carolina I'm Champion" kind of made sense to me. Or maybe they left out an apostrophe, a comma, *and* an *a*: "Carolina, I'm a Champion" would have made even more sense.

Whatever it was, I kept seeing them all over the place. I saw guys tossing Frisbees on Connor Beach wearing these shirts. I saw guys wearing them at Troll's bar. I saw guys wearing them at freshman orientation at Carmichael Auditorium. The thing I really liked about these shirts were the accessories that came with them. And when I say accessories, I mean girls. I never saw a guy wearing one who didn't have a girl walking with him and drinking Old Milwaukee with him.

I wanted a Carolina IM Champion T-shirt. I wanted one bad. I wanted one more than I wanted my diploma. I guess it was kind of silly to be so obsessed with a T-shirt, but I couldn't help it. If I had just been able to go to the student store and buy one, I probably wouldn't have wanted it. The fact that I couldn't have it made me want it more.

It was kind of like getting a varsity letter jacket in high school. I played football not because I liked playing football. I played football just so I could get a South Granville varsity jacket. The jacket was ugly, but I thought it was cool. I thought that I'd look cool wearing it and that Nancy Walsh and Susan Tuten would be fooled into thinking that I was a jock and they might actually give me some. Susan eventually did give me some, but it wasn't the jacket. It was the Jack Daniels. But that's a different story.

The more times that I was denied getting a shirt, the more I wanted one. I played coed intramural softball, men's softball, and flag football my freshman year. And none of these teams got anywhere near a winning season, much less a trophy T-shirt.

I went 0 for my sophomore year as well. In my junior year, we had a really good team and made it to the championship game of the men's softball tournament. Our Alexander dorm team faced Teague dorm in the final. Teague was the jock dorm on campus. They weren't varsity jocks, but they were the studs of intramurals. They even had a slogan: "Your mama sleeps in Teague." And it was probably true. Because every one of them had a Carolina IM Champion shirt. *Those motherfuckers.* And they all wore them in the game against us. It was completely intimidating. They all seemed to scream, "We're all Carolina Intramural Champions and you are not and never will be!" We lost 10–2.

I came very close to getting a shirt during summer school after my junior year. I kind of had a small crush on Katy Evans, a cute blonde from Pineville. She was in my Russian history class that summer and I ran into her at Linda's Bar one Thursday evening. She was very tanned and was wearing something that made her look extremely hot: a Carolina IM champion shirt. That's when my small crush turned into a major one. Somehow after a few beers, I found myself in her dorm room making out with her. Soon she was wearing nothing but the shirt and her panties. She reached for the bottom of her shirt to lift it off and I said, "Wait, keep the shirt on."

"No, I want to get naked," she said. She stripped her shirt off and tossed it into the darkness. We frolicked for a while, and the next thing I remember was Katy waking me and saying she was leaving for her eight-o'clock class.

"You can just let yourself out when you wake up, sleepy head." She kissed me on the cheek and left. I immediately opened my eyes and looked around the room. It took me two seconds to find it. There it was, sitting crumpled on top of a pile of dirty clothes. I jumped out of bed and grabbed it. I was standing there, naked, holding the shirt, and I was ecstatic. Not only had I just gotten action, I had gotten *the shirt*. I couldn't believe my luck. I quickly put it on and looked at myself in the mirror, expecting to see the reflection of a champion. What I saw was a large guy wearing a small shirt. I quickly took it off to look at the size: XS. *Damn.* I needed an XL. So close. I folded the shirt and left it on her bed. *Denied. Again.*

In the fall of my senior year, I played coed softball again. Finally, the stars aligned. Or should I say the goats aligned. In the championship game, we met a team from Granville Towers. With two outs in the bottom of the ninth, we were trailing 5–4. Adam Kandell was on third and Chris Dooley was on second. I came to bat and hit a dribbler down the first-base line. It was sure to be the final out of the game. But it went straight through Bill Buckner's legs and into the outfield. Adam and Chris both scored. When Chris crossed the plate, we celebrated like we had won the World Series, the Super Bowl and the Daytona 500 at the same time. We had won something much bigger. We had won Carolina IM Champion T-shirts. Finally.

After the game, Peggy, the intramural commissioner, brought a cardboard box over to our dugout. It was a box full of shirts. "Congrat-ulations, Alexander dorm, you are the Fall Coed Softball Intramural Champions," she said. "Here are your Intramural Champion shirts." She opened the box and started handing out the shirts. They were baby blue. They didn't have a Tar Heel on them. They said Carolina Intramural Champion but listed all the intramural sports in small letters underneath. This wasn't the shirt that I had obsessed about for the past three and a half years. This shirt *sucked*. It was lame.

It was like winning an Oscar and getting to the stage and having Julia Roberts hand you a Daytime Emmy.

Peggy the Commish said that they had changed the design of the shirts. "Isn't it awesome?" she said with a sense of pride that instantly revealed that it was she who had designed them.

"It's nice," I said, thinking that this was the biggest screw-up since New Coke was introduced.

But though I hated the shirts, there still was celebratory drinking to be done. We all put our newfangled shirts on and headed to Troll's for 25-cent PBRs. At Troll's we ran into Kevin O'Brien, the redheaded jackass vice president of Teague dorm, who happened to be wearing a Carolina IM Champion "classic" T-shirt.

"Nice shirt," O'Brien said to me. "What did you win? The gay Olympics?"

"No, we won the coed softball championship tonight," I said.

"That's the same shirt Greg Huge-anus wore after he won his diving medal, isn't it?"

O'Brien laughed and turned to talk with an obviously intoxicated Phi Mu. I asked our center fielder, Tommy Moser, if I could have a cigarette.

"You don't smoke," he said.

"I know, just give me one."

He handed me a Kool and lit it for me. I took a drag and thought,

How could anyone smoke this shit? I guess smokers need nicotine. I just needed fire on the end of a stick.

O'Brien still had his back to me, but his plastic cup of PBR was on the bar. It was full. I waited for him to take another swig. A minute later he did and put the cup back on the bar. It was about half full. I took another drag and while he wasn't looking, I pressed the lit end of the cigarette into his cup, right above the beer line. I removed the cigarette to reveal a perfect circle melted in the plastic.

"Let's walk over and stand by the door," I said to Tommy with a smile. We turned and watched O'Brien. He picked up his beer and as he took a drink, PBR flowed through the cigarette hole all over his shirt. He looked around for us, but as soon as we saw the beer flow, we headed out the door and laughed all the way to our favorite bar, He's Not Here. I felt pretty good about drenching O'Brien, but the truth is, he was right. The new shirts blew.

By the time that spring came around, I had pretty much resigned myself to the fact that I would graduate Carolina before I got one of the shirts. Especially since they had changed the design. But unbeknownst to me, just like when New Coke came out, there had been a public outcry to bring back the old shirts. They reintroduced the classic design for the spring champions.

Of course, we lost in the spring softball championship game and had to watch the Manly Men put on put on their classic Carolina IM Champion shirts on the field after the game. (Manly was the name of a dorm and they should have been given champion T-shirts just for their name. They could have been the Manly Marauders, the Manly Mammoths, or the Manly Mustangs. But to be able to say, "We're the Manly Men" was very clever. Even though they were a bunch of total douchebags. Mainly because they had those shirts and I didn't.)

I was so incensed that they had changed back to the original designs that I decided to do something about it. I went to the intramural offices at Woolen Gym. I took my baby blue intramural champion shirt with me. I talked with the director of intramurals, Sandra Blevins. She had taken Peggy's place in the spring. Apparently, Peggy had quit after they had gone back to the old T-shirt design. (She should have been fired.)

I asked Sandra a very simple question: "Could I trade my baby blue shirt for what I consider a real IM champion shirt?"

She had a simple reply: "No."

"What do you mean no?" I said. "We won the championship last fall. Why can't I have a real championship T-shirt?"

"The light blue shirt represents a fall '83 victory. These shirts represent spring '84 champions. It would be misleading for you to wear one of these."

She told me this as I was looking at three boxes full of these shirts. My first inclination was to just grab one and make a run for it. But I was scheduled to graduate in a month, and the thought of going through honor court wasn't very appealing.

So I said, "Why do you have so many shirts left? Aren't all the spring championships over?"

She said, "Yes, but we still have the Big Four Tournament."

"What's that?"

The Big Four Tournament was a competition that was held every spring between the Big Four universities in North Carolina: Wake Forest, Duke, NC State and UNC. The intramural champions in each sport from each school compete with each other to determine the Big Four Intramural champion. All of the students who compete in the Big Four Tournament get Carolina IM Champion T-shirts.

"So if we had beaten the Manly Men yesterday, we would have gotten shirts for winning the championship and *another* shirt if we competed in the Big Four Tournament?"

"Yes," she replied.

I was ready to shoot myself.

"You really must want one of these shirts," she said.

"Uh, yeah," I replied.

"Well, do you play golf?"

"Not very well," I said.

"That's too bad," she said, "because we don't have a golf team to compete in the Big Four tournament."

"When is it?" I asked.

"Tomorrow morning. It starts at seven a.m. at the Duke University Golf Club."

"And if I compete in it, no matter how we do, even if we come in fourth place, we get a shirt?"

"That's right," she said. "You will be representing UNC and for that you'll get a T-shirt."

"Count me in," I said, barely able to contain my glee. "I'll have three others join me and we'll do Carolina proud." It didn't bother me at all that I didn't have golf clubs and didn't know anyone who did.

"When do we get our shirts?" I asked.

"When you finish the round, come back here and I'll give them to you."

"Awesome."

I went back to Avery dorm and immediately called my cousin Ken Oakley. He said that he was in and that he could borrow clubs from Glen Sparrow. I borrowed a set of Lady Pings from Tammy Puckett. The clubs were great. The pink golf bag was even better. I saw Tommy Moser, the guy who'd let me borrow a cigarette the night before, leaving the dorm and I asked him to join us. He laughed and said he would love to. He asked Ken and me to come with him to Troll's and since it was Friday, we said we would love to. At Troll's, after our fourth pitcher of Meister Brau, we found our fourth. David Spencer was perfect because he actually played golf and owned his own clubs. Two sets in fact, and he agreed to let Tommy borrow his old set.

We spent the next few hours singing Hank Junior, swilling swill, and laughing about our good fortune. Who would have thunk it? After four years of trying to win that stupid shirt, all we had to do to get one was go hack it up on a golf course for a few hours. This was the best ever. We closed Troll's down and stumbled back to the dorm around two a.m.

Thank goodness I remembered to set my alarm. 5:45 a.m. came around very quickly. I climbed out of bed and called the boys. Spencer picked us up at six fifteen in front of the dorm. We threw our clubs in the trunk and went straight to the Bojangles' drive-through for some Cajun Filet Biscuits. We figured if we were going to be golf champions, we'd better start with a good breakfast.

We were still a bit drunk from the night before, but it was only an eight-mile drive to the Duke campus. We had no idea where the Duke University Golf Club was and we figured we could just drive around until we found it. We found it at 6:55. We didn't think that was a problem at all since we thought that the golfers from the other schools could go ahead and start. Ken, Spencer, Tommy, and I would play in the last foursome. Or so we thought.

As soon as Spencer put the car in Park, someone yelled, "The Carolina team is here. We need you guys on the first tee." We piled out of the car. We were a motley crew to say the least. I looked semi-golf-er-like with khakis and a golf shirt. But my Chuck Taylor sneakers were a dead giveaway that I was no Nicklaus. Ken was wearing a Grateful Dead tie-dye shirt, shorts, and black Nike basketball shoes. Spencer was the only one who was wearing golf shoes. But Tommy was wearing something that I don't think these folks had ever seen on a golf course: black skin. (I think Tiger Woods was probably eight years old at the time.) Tommy was also wearing a Douglas Byrd High

School football jersey over a collared shirt. His Earth, Wind & Fire–style afro bulged out from under his LA Rams baseball cap.

As we walked up to the tee box, I got a case of cottonmouth so bad that I felt like I needed to shave my tongue. Surrounding the first tee was a gallery of at least seventy-five people. The other schools had fans. We made our way through the crowd to the starter.

"Which one of you is playing first?" the starter asked.

"We're going to play together," I said.

"Son, this is a tournament. One player from each of the schools will make up a foursome," he said.

I swallowed hard as I looked across the tee box and saw the other teams. The NC State players all were wearing tan khakis and red Wolfpack polos. The Duke players had matching white polos and dark blue slacks. The Wake players had gold golf shirts and black pants. And they all had Rodney Dangerfield *Caddyshack*-style golf bags. But these guys were so uptight, I can guarantee you that there was no keg in any of their bags.

I looked over at my team and said, "Who wants to bat leadoff?" Ken said he would since he usually batted leadoff on our softball team. So Ken stepped up to the first tee and introduced himself to the other guys. He was the first of his group to tee off. Ken placed the ball on the tee and took a couple of practice swings. His form looked good to me. Then he stepped up to the ball and swung. The ball went straight. Straight sideways through the gallery and about seventy-five yards deep in the woods. Thank goodness it didn't kill anyone. Ken turned to the crowd, tipped his cap and said, "Well I'm glad I got that one out of my system."

The Wake, State, and Duke guys each stepped up and hit 250-yard drives right down the middle. Ken hit a provisional shot about twenty feet past the ladies' tees. He walked down to his ball and hit it again. By the time he was even with the other players he was on his fifth shot.

Spencer, Tommy, and I were cracking up on the outside, but on the inside we were freaking out, because we, or at least I, knew that we weren't any better than Ken.

But I guess pressure players play well when the pressure is on. Spencer put his first ball in play. Tommy knocked the shit out of the ball. It must have gone 300 yards and split the fairway. Mouths dropped in the gallery—I'm still not sure if it was because of his shot or because they had never seen a black man who wasn't a caddy. My first shot did not win long drive of the day. I topped the ball and it literally went about three inches in front of the tee. I bent down to pick it up, but Biff from Wake said, "Don't touch it. You have to play it from there."

I turned to him and said, "Are you shitting me? Don't I get two swings on the first tee?"

"No," he replied. "This is a tournament. It's not putt-putt."

"Oh really?" I said as I reached into my pink golf bag and got my putter. I stepped up to the ball and took a full putter swing and slapped the ball a hundred yards down the fairway. *Game on.*

For the next five hours I played the golf game of my life. And this was without any gimme putts. The jackasses made me putt everything. Even if the ball was less than five feet from the cup. Can you imagine? I shot a 70 on the front nine and got hot on the back and shot a 65. My 135 total was good for 4th place in my foursome. Biff shot a 79, Howard from Duke shot an 81, and Dick from NC State shot an 84.

On the eighteenth green, Ken, Spencer, and Moser were waiting and watching as I finished my round with another five-putt. When my last eight-inch putt sank, I shook hands with Biff, Howard, and Dick and walked off the green with the look of a champion. Because finally, I was: a Carolina IM Champion. And so were Ken, Spencer, and Tommy Moser. As we carried our bags to the car, Spencer told me he shot a 93, Tommy shot a 107 and Ken shot a 147. Our combined score was 492. Only 180 shots behind the Wake Forest team. Good for 4th place. And good for 4 Carolina IM Champion T-shirts.

We drove straight back to Chapel Hill, stopping only at the Wilco to pick up a twelve-pack of Milwaukee's Best and a pouch of Levi Garrett. Some people light a championship cigar; I preferred a chaw of championship chew.

When we got to Woolen Gym, Sandra was in her office waiting for us. (Okay, she wasn't really waiting for us, but she was in her office.) We told her we just finished competing in the Big Four Championship. She asked if we had our scorecards. My heart sank because I knew that I didn't bring it. Ken smiled, reached into his back pocket, and handed it to Sandra. She glanced at it and said, "Clearly, you aren't golfers. But you represented UNC, and for that you are Carolina IM Champions." She reached into the box with the shirts and said, "What size do you guys wear?" She handed each of us a shirt and we immediately put them on. Then we quickly got out of there before she changed her mind.

I felt different as soon as I put it on. It was like wearing a license to talk shit. An ear-to-ear grin stretched across my face. As I walked from Woolen Gym back to Avery Dorm, I felt the stares of attractive coeds and envious wannabes. I nodded and grinned at each of them. Even Betsy Buche, the hottest girl in Avery, smiled as I strutted past her. When I got back to my room, I closed the door and stood in front of the full-length mirror to take a gander at what everyone had just seen for the first time. There I was, at long last, wearing a Carolina IM Champion T-shirt. With a big piece of chewing tobacco stuck between my front teeth.

This is me wearing the Carolina IM Champion shirt for the first time (check out the babes it attracted).

PATHETIC STICK FIGURES

PEOPLE OFTEN ASK ME HOW I GOT INTO ADVERTISING. Or more specifically, how I knew that I wanted to work in advertising. Was there an aha moment where I suddenly saw the light (or the dark, depending on your view of this business)? Every time I'm asked this, I answer with a definitive yes. And my thoughts go back to a rainy Sunday afternoon in Chapel Hill.

I was a senior at Carolina, one month away from earning that damn T-shirt, and two months away from graduating with a degree in Industrial Relations. Almost thirty years have passed since then, and I still can't tell you exactly what that degree was about. I think it had something to do with labor management. Dealing with unions and the like. I really can't say that I chose that major. It chose me. Simply because I didn't want to take the accounting courses required to get a business degree. Accounting wasn't a requirement for Industrial Relations. I was twenty-one, and I was lazy. In my mind, it didn't matter what the diploma said, as long as I got one. Oddly enough, I was right. But at the time I had no clue what I was going to do after I wore my cap and gown on May 11.

That dreary afternoon, I drove over to Carolina Apartments in Carrboro to study with my good friend Laura Bowen. Laura had lived down the hall from me at Avery Dorm the year before, and she was always good at giving me advice about girls. I carried my Econ 157 book and assignments upstairs to her place, even though I wasn't necessarily planning to study. I just wanted to shoot the shit with her for a while. But Laura, who had a 4.0 GPA, had other plans. She had a project due the next day and needed to get some work done. She basically told me to sit on the couch and shut up. So I started reading chapter after scintillating chapter of economic theory.

Just as I was falling into a midafternoon slumber, I looked over at Laura working on her homework. She was drawing little stick figure guys on paper and writing captions beneath them. I thought, *That girl has no artistic talent at all. She couldn't draw a card in a poker game.*

"What are you doing?" I said with the artistic arrogance that only a son of two potters could muster.

She looked up from her masterpiece and said, "I'm doing my Journalism 170 homework."

"Your homework is drawing pathetic stick figures?"

She laughed. "I'm coming up with a new ad campaign for the Pillsbury Doughboy."

I closed my econ book and walked over to the table where she was working. I looked at her sketches and said, "You actually get college credit for this?"

"Yes, and I've got an A in the class."

"That is sooooo easy."

"It's not really that easy, David."

"It's a lot easier than economics," I argued.

"Well it's not a slide, I can tell you that. Professor Sweeney is really tough," Laura said, a little bit defensively.

I wasn't trying to be a smart aleck. I was genuinely amazed that a course in advertising even existed. It had never occurred to me that someone actually wrote those jingles on TV. That someone actually created those hilarious *Tastes great, Less filling* commercials. And more importantly, that someone actually got *paid* to do it. To say I was intrigued would be putting it mildly.

"So tell me about Dr. Sweeney," I said to Laura.

"Well first of all, he's not a doctor. He's been at Carolina for I think four years. Every year he has won the award as the most popular professor in the J-School. Before he came here, he worked at a famous ad agency in Chicago—Foote, Cone & Belding."

"Isn't that where Darrin Stephens worked?"

"No, fool, that was McMann & Tate." Laura giggled. "Anyway, he was a copywriter there and was on some really big accounts, like Raid and Sears."

"That's cool."

"He wrote the Raid *Kills Bugs Dead* commercials and some Sears Die Hard battery commercials."

"Really?"

"Remember the Die Hard commercial where they parked all those cars in Yankee Stadium and left their lights on overnight? The next morning all of the cars that didn't have Die Hard batteries were dead and the Die Hard car started with no problem?"

"Yeah," I said, "and I remember the line, 'The Sears Die Hard: The only battery to bat 1000 at Yankee Stadium.'"

"That's it."

"Sweeney wrote that? Wow, that's really cool." I was impressed. I think Laura could tell.

"If you're seriously interested, you should go talk with him. He's really nice. His office is in the basement of Carroll Hall."

For a college student who had all of the drive of a two-cylinder Yugo, showing up for class was an accomplishment. Showing up to talk with a professor was completely uncharted territory. But there I found myself first thing Monday morning, standing patiently outside his locked office, waiting for the Die Hard battery guy to arrive before his nine-o'clock class. I wondered what he would look like. I pictured a crusty guy in his early fifties. I was close. He was a crusty guy in his early thirties. He walked around me, clutching a briefcase and wearing a London Fog raincoat. His other hand was fumbling in his pocket for his keys. He found them, unlocked his door, and without looking up said, "Can I help you?"

"Are you Professor Sweeney?" I asked, nervously.

"Yes," he said as he hung his coat and unpacked his briefcase. He wore tiny wire-rim glasses, had curly dark hair like someone had just given him a perm, and a gap between his front teeth. My first impression was that he was a cross between David Letterman and Greg Brady. He sat down in his desk chair, looked up at me and said, "And who are you?"

"I'm David Oakley and I'm interested in advertising. I'd like to talk with you about taking your Intro to Advertising class."

"OK, what year are you? Freshman . . . sophomore?"

"I'm a senior."

"So you're graduating in two months?"

"Yes."

"You probably should think about getting a job. What's your major?"

"Industrial Relations." The puzzled look he gave me showed that he knew even less than I did about Industrial Relations.

"Well you should try to get a job in whatever type of work you get with that major."

"But I want to get a job in advertising."

"I don't want this to sound harsh, but I'm going to be real with you. There are very few jobs in advertising. Especially for beginners. Two, maybe three students graduating from J-school this year will get jobs at agencies. It's super competitive. Your best bet would be to get your diploma in May and use it to get a job."

"But I really want to be in advertising."

"A lot of people do," he said, as he grabbed a notebook and a copy of *Adweek*. "I've got to teach my nine o'clock. It was nice to meet you.

Good luck." He ushered me out of his office and locked the door behind us.

I stood and watched him walk down the hall away from me and I thought, *Man, he's not anywhere near as nice as Laura said he was.*

Little did I know it, but I had just met my mentor.

The next two months passed quickly. Graduation came and went. I got a job waiting tables and an apartment in Chapel Hill with a couple of friends who weren't so ready to enter the real world either. I was having fun. But I couldn't get my conversation with Sweeney off my mind. I found it hard to believe that there was no possibility of me having a career in advertising. And having some hotshot professor/ex-ad guy tell me I couldn't do it made me want it even more.

The day before summer school classes started, I went to see Sweeney again. I really didn't have a plan on what I'd say, I just figured I'd tell him again how much I was interested in advertising and maybe, just maybe, he'd let me take his class.

When I got to his office I could see him through the opaque glass in his door typing on his electric Smith Corona. I knocked twice and saw him get up from his desk. He opened the door and looked at me. He recognized me, but I could tell he didn't know from where.

"Hi, Professor Sweeney, remember me? I'm David Oakley. I spoke with you a couple of months ago about taking your class." I could see the wheels turning in his head and he nodded in the affirmative.

"I thought you graduated."

"I did. But um, I'm still living in Chapel Hill, and I'd thought maybe I could take your class in the first summer school session."

"But…you graduated."

"That doesn't mean that I should stop learning."

He smiled and said, "Good point, but if you graduated you're not enrolled in school, right?"

"True, but I could register for summer school. You know,

continuing education," I said with a grin.

"Well, even if you did register, there are seventy students already enrolled in my class. And fifteen more on the waiting list. There's just no room for you."

My heart hit the floor. I had finally figured out what I wanted to do with my life and I was being told no again. The man behind the Raid campaign was killing my dream, dead.

What I said next truly amazed me and probably totally freaked Sweeney out. "Well, Professor Sweeney, I know you're a great professor and your classes are very popular. I know you have a stranglehold on the annual Professor of the Year award. But I also know college students. And college students sometimes get sick and miss class. Sometimes college students even skip classes. Even when it's their favorite class. And their favorite professor. Believe it or not, Professor Sweeney, students sometimes have better things to do than go to your class. And I'll guarantee you that every single day you teach, all seventy seats will not be full. Every day, for one reason or another, there will be one empty seat. And you know who's going to be sitting in that empty seat? Me. I'll be there. Because I want to learn about advertising. See you next Monday. In class."

I turned and left his office. And this time, he stood at his door and watched me walk down the hall.

I have no idea what he was thinking. *Maybe this kid is the next David Ogilvy.* Or more likely, the next David Berkowitz.

The following Monday, I walked into Carroll Hall and found the J-170 classroom. Class was scheduled to begin at nine thirty and I waited in the hall

FOR THOSE OF YOU YOUNGER THAN 50, DAVID BERKOWITZ IS THE INFAMOUS SON OF SAM SERIAL KILLER WHO TERRORIZED NEW YORK CITY IN THE LATE 1970'S. FOR THOSE OF YOU LUCKY ENOUGH NOT TO BE IN THE BUSINESS OF ADVERTISING, DAVID OGILVY IS THE FOUNDER OF OGILVY, ONE OF THE BIGGEST ADVERTISING AGENCIES IN THE WORLD.

as student after student filed in and took their seats. *Holy Moly,* I thought, *this guy IS popular.* I started getting nervous. Maybe there won't be any empty seats. Sweeney walked over to the front of the class and said, "Welcome to Journalism 170. This will be like no journalism class you have ever taken."

A second later, I spotted a girl wearing Kappa Kappa Gamma jersey stand up and head for the door, leaving an open seat in the second-to-last row. I hustled over and sat down.

I repeated this ritual every day for the next four weeks. I always got a seat. It actually became easier as the weeks went on. Even more people than I thought would skip, skipped. On Wednesday of the fourth week, we were scheduled to have a midterm exam. I studied like I'd never studied before and came prepared to take the exam, even though I'd never even registered for the class. That morning Sweeney strolled into class and said, "Remove everything but your pencil from your desk," and he walked around the room and placed an exam on each student's desk. When he got to my desk he stopped. He looked at me, sighed, and gave me a half-smile. Then he plopped an exam down in front of me and said, "OK, you're in."

That's how I got into advertising. Well, actually that's how I got into my first advertising class. I had overcome a major obstacle just to get in. The obstacle wasn't Sweeney. He never stopped me. He just questioned how badly I wanted it. The obstacle was me. It was up to me to show how much I wanted it. And I proved it. I made it happen all on my own.

I sat there for a moment and proudly looked around the classroom, basking in the glory of passing my first test in advertising. Then I stopped congratulating myself and started taking the exam.

HERSHEY RAPPER

I THINK I NOW HOLD AN ADVERTISING WORLD RECORD. No, not for the worst ad book or for the most self-centered ad book. I am convinced that I now own the record for the longest time between coming up with an advertising idea and actually presenting it to a client: **25 years, 3 months, and 17 days.**

It all started in John Sweeney's Advanced Copywriting class at Carolina. Before I go too far in this story, I have to ask the question: How could there be an Advanced Copywriting class at college? I guess they figured that if you passed Introduction to Copywriting, you were ready to become an advanced copywriter. We skipped right over So-So Copywriter, Mediocre Copywriter, and Run-of-the-Mill Copywriter. (Not to worry though, I did all of those once I got a real job.) Even though I made an A in Advanced Copywriting, I still wouldn't call myself an advanced copywriter. But this really has nothing to do with the story, aside from the fact that I'm trying to increase the word count of this book. (And I'm doing a damn good job of it, if I do say so myself.)

Every year in the Advanced Copywriting class (which I was taking post-graduation, while waiting tables), Sweeney's students were given an assignment from a real advertising agency. Our class was briefed by Ogilvy & Mather New York. Our task was to come up with an advertising campaign for one of their clients: Hershey. Specifically, the Hershey's Kiss. The brief was simple: *The Hershey's Kiss is a great-tasting chocolate treat in a small size that can be enjoyed the whole year 'round.*

Three weeks later, the creative director from Ogilvy came to Chapel Hill to see our work. (As I recall, he was an advanced copywriter.) Before presenting my work, I was more nervous than usual, because my presentation involved me rapping.

I am a horrible rapper, but an even worse singer. I'm totally tone-deaf. So I convinced myself that I was a better rapper than a singer. This somehow gave me the courage to stand up in front of our class and the guy from Ogilvy and introduce a character that I called The Hershey Rapper. Yes, a rapping chocolate Kiss.

I held up my crudely drawn picture of the Hershey Rapper.

I pictured him as a cross between a California Raisin and Run from Run DMC.

And then I started rapping.

I'm the Hershey Rapper,
Ya think I'm just foil.
I cover the sweetest kiss in the world.
You rip me off with such great haste,
Just to get to that amazin' Hershey taste.
I said, Kiss ka kiss ka kiss ka kiss kiss kiss.

You like me at Christmas,
But I'm a candy for all seasons,
Listen to this, I'll tell you the reason.
Big chocolate in a little size,
The Hershey Rapper tells no lies.
You want a Kiss ka kiss ka kiss ka kiss kiss kiss.

The Hershey Rapper.
The Big Taste. For the Big Place. In the Middle of your Face!

As soon as I was finished, the room exploded in laughter. It was one of those moments where I wasn't quite sure whether they were laughing with me, or at me. The guy from Ogilvy clapped his hands three times and said, "I certainly have never seen anything like that."

"So you like it?" I asked, apprehensively.

"I love it. I don't know that Hershey would like it, but I love it."

That was good enough for me. This guy was giving out the grades on this assignment, and if I got an A, I couldn't care less what Hershey thought of it. Not only did I get an A, but I got an interview with the head of recruitment at Ogilvy. I didn't get a job at Ogilvy, but soon after that, I rapped my way through twelve interviews in one day at Young & Rubicam. Amazingly, they hired me. On one condition: that I never rap again. The Hershey Rapper helped me land my first job.

As the years passed, I couldn't help but occasionally wonder what

Hershey would have thought about the idea. That guy was probably right, but I've seen a lot of ad people be wrong about their clients. So I vowed to myself that if I ever got the chance to meet with Hershey, I was going to present the Hershey Rapper.

Which brings me to 2012. Greg Johnson, the chief marketing officer at BooneOakley, and I were flying from Charlotte to Hershey, Pennsylvania, to do a capabilities presentation. A capabilities presentation is simply a meeting to show a potential client what an agency is known for and is qualified to do. Little did the folks at Hershey know that our capabilities included rapping.

I talked it over with Greg at the airport to get a gauge of whether or not to show "The Hershey Rapper" to them. I hadn't even convinced myself we should show it, but I really wanted Greg to say it was OK. After all, we were meeting with them to seriously try to win a piece of business. Not to satisfy some strange whim that I had.

Greg looked at me like I had lost what little was left of my mind.

"Hey, it's your agency…" he said in a way that wasn't exactly confidence-building. Then he grinned and continued, "It's not like this would blow the account for us. We don't have it. Read the room. And if things are going well, I say start rapping."

"Cool," I replied. "If things aren't going well, I'll just stop before I get to the Hershey Rapper slide."

As we got there and the meeting progressed, it was hard to determine whether or not to do the rap. The meeting was going well, but it didn't feel like we were blowing them away.

I started thinking that maybe the rap bit would be better shown on our fourth or fifth meeting with them. After we had gotten to know them a bit better and they were more comfortable with us. But then it occurred to me that we might not even get a *second* meeting. So if I was ever going to do the Hershey rap for Hershey, this was my chance.

I still wasn't sure whether or not I was going to present it until Greg was wrapping (not rapping) up the meeting. "I want to thank you guys for taking the time out of your busy schedules to meet with us today. Honestly, it's an honor and privilege to be able to show our capabilities to you. Hershey is the type of company that BooneOakley would be passionate about and would love to partner with. You've been on our target list since BooneOakley was founded eleven years ago. In fact, Dave has wanted to meet with Hershey even longer than that. What is it now, Dave? Twenty-five years?"

I smiled. Greg had just given me the green light.

"Yes, it's been twenty-five years. Thanks for reminding everyone how old I am," I joked. "Anyway, when I was in college I took an advanced copywriting class. One of our assignments was to come up with a campaign for the Hershey's Kiss. And I always said that if I ever had a meeting with Hershey, I was going to present this idea."

One of the Hershey guys said, "So this is the big closer?"

"Yeah, Greg thinks it's going to be a closer: like you guys close the door behind us, bolt it shut, and never want to see us again."

"You guys have done well so far. Don't blow it."

Greg clicked the PowerPoint and the Hershey Rapper was on the 50-inch plasma screen right behind me.

"This is...the Hershey Rapper," I said. "He's kind of a cross between Run DMC and the California Raisins. And twenty-five years ago, I thought that a rapping Hershey's Kiss would be an amazing tool to sell chocolate." I motioned to the crudely drawn character on the screen behind me, "Aren't those illustrations awesome? I did them myself."

"Amazing," one of them said, facetiously.

"But the rap is even better. Want me to rap it?"

"You have to now," Beth, the director of procurement chimed in.

"OK, here goes." And I started rapping.

As soon as I was finished, laughter filled the room. Eric Lent from Hershey clapped his hands and said, "That is something else."

"So you like it?" I again asked apprehensively.

"How can you not like that?" said Eric.

I wasn't really sure if he was joking until a week later. That's when we got the call that told us we had been selected as a finalist to become Hershey's digital agency of record.

So it turns out, I could have waited until the next meeting to perform the Hershey Rapper. But maybe if I hadn't done the Hershey Rapper there never would have been a second meeting. Either way, I just set a new world record.

The most important lesson of this book just might be: "You may never get a second meeting."

"YOU MAY NEVER GET A SECOND MEETING.

One of my mentors, Peter Coughter, a former colleague at The Martin Agency and a former Providence College basketball star, told me before we walked in to pitch the Charlotte Hornets' business, "Play your game. But most importantly, leave it all on the court." Spoken like a true coach. I think of his words before every presentation. You never want to leave a meeting and say to yourself, "Man, I wish I'd done this, or I wish I'd done that." I think Nike says it best: *Just Do It.*

WANT TO BE A COPYWRITER? LEARN TO SPELL

I FOUND SOMETHING SPECIAL IN OUR ATTIC RECENTLY: AN OLD SPIRAL-BOUND UNC NOTEBOOK. It instantly took me back to a time when I was obsessed with getting my first job as an advertising copywriter.

Inside were two dozen Wite-Out–dotted letters that I had typed on my Smith Corona. I had painstakingly pecked each one out twenty-five years ago, to send to creative directors at the best agencies in the country.

Reading them for the first time in a quarter century, I was particularly impressed by my poignant letter to Lee Clow.

That is, until I noticed how I spelled his name. Well, at least now I know why he never wrote back.

WITE-OUT LOOKS LIKE IT'S MISSPELLED, DOESN'T IT? WELL IT'S NOT. I LOOKED IT UP.

■ DAVID OAKLEY

```
                              6118-A Shanda Drive
                              Raleigh NC 27609
                              February 12, 1987


Lee Chow
Executive Creative Director
Chiat/Day, Inc.
517 S. Olive St.
Los Angeles, CA  90013


Dear Lee:

I guess its a little odd to be getting a letter from a perfect
stranger, so let me introduce myself.  I am a student who has
just finished the advertising program at the University of
North Carolina at Chapel Hill.  I am also very interested in
writing for Chiat/Day.

I would really appreciate it if you would take a look at the
ads that I have enclosed.  Any comments or suggestions on
how to improve them would be greatly appreciated.  I will
call you on Friday, February 20 to get your opinion.

I realize that I only sent you a small sample of my work.
If you like what you see, I will be happy to send you the
rest of my book.  Or better yet, we can set up an interview.

Thank you very much for taking the time to look at my work.


                    Sincerely:


                    David Oakley
```

I really could have used a proofreader—too bad 123hire.com didn't exist back then.

PART ƎƎЯHꓕ
TO THE BIG APPLE AND BACK

EVERYONE NEEDS TO LIVE IN NEW YORK CITY AT SOME POINT IN THEIR LIFE. After submitting my portfolio to dozens of agencies, I finally got my first job at Young & Rubicam. I moved to the big city after studying with John Sweeney, expecting to stay for two years, tops. I stayed for almost eight. The next few stories are about life in the city and some of the things I learned working at Y&R and TBWA in New York, and one of the main reasons that I came back South. Let's just say it involves a crowded elevator.

Even though I was fortunate enough to be a part of the iconic Absolut Vodka print campaign when I was in NYC, my career really began to take off after I moved back to North Carolina. I started doing better work and won a few awards. I also found that office politics and bad clients were not exclusive to the big New York shops and that going to strip clubs is an activity best enjoyed out of town. Plus one essential lesson for everyone in advertising: Your most important client is yourself.

CAN I SEE YOUR BOOK?

LESS THAN A YEAR AFTER STARTING MY FIRST JOB AS A COPY-WRITER AT YOUNG & RUBICAM IN NEW YORK, I FOUND MYSELF INTERVIEWING FOR MY JOB AGAIN. But this time it wasn't just me interviewing. It was our entire creative group.

First day on the job as a copywriter. You would think an internationally known advertising powerhouse like Y&R could do a better job cropping their ID cards.

Y&R had just brought in Mike Robertson, a hot creative director from a smaller shop, and was paying him a not-so-small fortune to right the ship.

At the time, Y&R was having such a hard time competing in the advertising industry award shows that they had started the OUR Awards. The best ad from Y&R each month won an award and was displayed in the seventh-floor lobby. I thought it was really lame that we had our own award show. Well, that is, until I won a month. Not only did the monthly OUR Award winner have their ad displayed in the lobby, but they got a $100 gift certificate for dinner and two tickets to a Broadway show. That was the thing about Y&R. The perks were awesome. The work? Not so much.

On his first day at Y&R, Mike Robertson called a meeting of our thirty-two-person creative group. He said, "I was hired to bring the glory back to Y&R. I want our work to rival the work that is coming out of Cliff Freeman, Ammirati & Puris, and Chiat/Day. We can do award-winning work at Y&R."

I was really excited by his words because I loved the Wendy's, BMW, and NYNEX Yellow Pages work those creatively driven shops were doing. The work coming out of Y&R at the time could be summarized in one word: boring.

"Doing great work is no small task for a 1,400-person shop," Mike continued, "But if we have the right people on board, we can do it. Over the next two weeks, I'd like for each of you to schedule a thirty-minute appointment with me. It will be a chance for me to get to know each of you and see the kind of work you've been doing. So bring your book. My assistant Linda has the appointment calendar. Please stop by her desk and sign up for a time to see me." Then he buttoned his Armani suit and walked away to his corner office.

My excitement quickly waned when I looked around the room and saw thirty-two slack-jawed writers and art directors. There were art directors who had been at Y&R for twenty-five years. Copywriters who had been working on Winston for the past twenty years. Some didn't even have a book anymore. It was the first time that I had ever seen creative people frightened. The meeting broke up and we adjourned to our offices. And that's where the chatter began.

"This guy is a hatchet man. He fired half the staff at Geer Dubois."

"My art director friend told me what he did at Scali: total massacre."

"He looks nice, but he's nothing but a cold-blooded killer. Better start looking for another job, Oakley."

It had taken me over a year of sending Xeroxed copies of my book to countless agencies to find my first job. I couldn't lose it after six months. Or could I? Suddenly, I was scared shitless. Mike Robertson was brought in to do one thing: clean house. Why in the world would he keep a junior writer from Granville County, North Carolina?

I went and made my appointment with Linda for the following Tuesday at nine thirty. I had four days to get my book together. That wasn't really all that hard to do, since it hadn't changed one bit since I got the job. In other words, I hadn't produced anything yet.

Tuesday arrived quickly, and I took my portfolio over to Mike's corner office. I kept telling myself that my book was good enough to get a job at Y&R, so it should be good enough to keep one. But I was just trying to make myself feel better. I was petrified. About the only thing I figured I had in my favor was that I was only making $18,000 a year. They wouldn't really save much money by firing me.

"Mike will see you now," Linda said, as she opened the door to his office.

As I stepped inside, Mike said "Hi, c'mon in."

"I'm David Oakley." I stuck out my hand and shook his.

"Oh, I know who you are," he said. But it was pretty obvious that he didn't. "You're a junior copywriter, right?"

"Yes," I replied. "I was hired as a part of Y&R's copy trainee program."

"Yes. Not many agencies do those programs anymore. They prefer to hire writers with experience."

I swallowed hard and all I could say was, "Oh."

"Well, let me take a look at your portfolio."

Mike flipped through the large black binder-type portfolio case, and after looking at a few of my ads said, "I like the drawings. Are you sure you're not an art director?"

I laughed because I had drawn everything in my book with colored pencils. At best they were on second-grade level.

He spent a few more minutes flipping through the book and when he finished looking at the last ad, he closed the book and looked at me.

"So...what do you think?" I said.

"Obviously you're a beginner. But your book isn't bad. I can see that you have some talent."

I can't believe Y&R hired me with this ad in my book.

"Thanks," I said. "I appreciate you taking the time to look at my stuff."

"No problem," he said as he turned to walk back toward his desk.

I said to his back, "Can I see *your* book?"

Mike spun around and looked at me with an eyebrow raised so high it almost reached his bald spot. "You want to see my book? My book?" he said gesturing to his chest. "You want to see *my* book?" he repeated.

"Well, yeah. I know about the print ad you did for Marriott. I saw it in Communication Arts. But that's really all I know about you except that you're my new creative director."

He turned and strode over toward his desk. He reached behind a filing cabinet and pulled out the biggest black portfolio case I had ever seen. He walked back over to me and put the case in front of me on the coffee table.

"No one has ever asked me to see my book," he said, as he plopped the portfolio on the coffee table.

"I just wanted to know more about the guy that I'll be working for…or won't be working for," I said acknowledging that I may have pushed it a little far with my request.

He laughed uneasily and said, "No, if you want to see my book, I should show you my book." He opened the case and showed me some print work for Perdue Chicken that he had done at Scali, McCabe, Sloves. I had seen them in the awards annuals. He took me through his work piece by piece, just the way I had taken him through my work. It was good—a lot better than I expected, actually.

When we got to the last ad, Mike looked up at me and asked, "So, what'd you think?"

"Not bad," I replied. "But I can see you have talent."

I smiled and thanked him for showing me his portfolio and told him that I looked forward to working with him. He smiled and said that he was glad that he was up to my standards.

As soon as I left Mike's office, I saw my friend Joe Green, a senior writer.

"How'd it go?" Joe asked, eagerly.

"OK, I guess."

"Did he like your work?"

"He liked some of it. I liked his work too."

"What do you mean you liked *his* work? Did he show it to you?"

"Yes, I asked to see it. I wanted to know what kind of work he had done."

"You asked to see his book?"

"Yeah," I said, not thinking that it was that big of a deal.

"Holy shit, you asked Mike Robertson to see his book?" Within minutes Joe had told everyone in the department that I had asked Mike to see his book.

"Oakley, I hope you have a headhunter. You just signed your death warrant."

Over the next two months, twenty-four of the thirty-two creatives in our group were let go. I wasn't one of them. I'd like to think that Mike kept me because he liked my work. But I'm pretty sure it was because I asked to see his.

Much later I realized that I had inadvertently taught myself a valuable lesson. When someone interviews you for a job, always remember to interview them back.

MEETING THE FOUNDERS OF YOUNG & RUBICAM

B *EEEEEEP. BEEEEEEP.* I opened my eyes and my digital Zenith clock radio was staring back at me: 7:45 a.m. I climbed out of bed, showered quickly and got dressed. Half an hour later, I was on the number 6 train heading downtown. I had a big meeting that morning. At ten thirty, I was scheduled to present Rolaids print ad ideas to my creative director and I wanted to get to Young & Rubicam early to prepare for my presentation.

I had been a copywriter for less than six months at the time, and I wanted to make a good impression. I grabbed a bagel and a cup of coffee from Vinnie's on 41st and was in my Madison Avenue office by eight forty-five. Plenty of time to get ready. I looked through my concepts and was deciding on the best order to show them in. The ads were designed to introduce new fruit-flavored Rolaids. Should I start with "Do Your Stomach a Flavor" or "Heavy Duty Goes Fruity"? I decided they were both so good that it didn't matter what I showed first. I was about to be on the fast track at Y&R. With headlines like those, I wouldn't be making $18,000 a year for long.

Then a strange thing happened. My office phone rang. It was odd that it rang, because no one in the creative department ever arrived before ten o'clock. Except for maybe the support staff. I answered, "Hello?"

"Dave," said the voice on the line. I immediately recognized it as Dave Shih's voice. Dave was my good friend and fellow copywriter at Y&R. I yelled "D to the fourth power, baby!" into the receiver. I knew that would crack him up, but he didn't laugh. He just said "Dave" again.

"What's your deal? Are you too hungover to talk?"

"We're in trouble," he said.

"For what?"

"Last night."

"Last night?" I responded, trying unsuccessfully to recall just what he was talking about.

"Ken Kadet just called me and said that Brian Knob wanted to know who number 12 and number 00 were on the Y&R softball team." Ken Kadet was the creative department manager and was like a den mother to the creatives. Brian Knob was another story. He was the worldwide chairman of Y&R. I'd never met him and had only seen his picture in the Y&R handbook. "He wants to see us in his office at nine o'clock."

"Well, we did have a couple of hits each last night. Maybe he wants to congratulate us."

"You're an idiot, Oakley. Victory Café…?"

My mind went back to the night before…

Around one fifteen a.m., Dave Shih and I had found ourselves in a corner booth in a little yuppie hangout on the Upper East Side. The place was called the Victory Café, which was an odd place to be dining, since three hours earlier we had lost our advertising league softball game 15–6. We ordered a plate of chicken wings and two Budweiser drafts. Our waiter was a guy named Steve, or that's what we figured his name was because he was wearing a Steve nametag. Not that he'd introduced himself or anything. Judging from our level of service, he was doing his utmost to completely avoid us. And who could blame him? We were just a couple of sweaty guys who had just played a softball game. Steve was much more interested in the two tables of Madonna wannabes sitting near the window.

Eventually our food and beers came, but we had to get up and go to the bar and get our own silverware. The wings were pretty good and the beer was cold. So we had no complaints about the food. But ol' Steve never brought us the bill. We must have sat there for 20 minutes with empty glasses when Dave asked, "You ever dined and dashed?"

"No, have you?"

"No, but I think this is a good of a time as any."

The next thing I knew I was sprinting down 3rd Avenue, trying to keep up with Dave. He turned left and headed west on 93rd Street, and when he got to Lexington Avenue he stopped and waited for me.

"Check that one off your list. Now you've dined and dashed, Oakley," Dave yelled as I huffed my way up the hill. We high-fived and caught our breath. We walked a couple more blocks laughing about how Steve probably still hadn't noticed we had left.

"How easy was that?"

"Like taking candy from a baby, baby."

"We'll have to do this more often."

"Every night, baby."

"That's how we'll survive in New York making $18,000 a year."

"Survive? That's how we'll thrive, baby." Dave said *baby* a lot. I think it was because Ray Charles said, *"You've got the right one, baby,"* in a Pepsi commercial that was running a lot in 1989. When we got to 95th Street, we parted ways. I went to my apartment on 95th and he headed to his on 97th.

"Good night, see you at the office in the morning."

As he walked toward the 96th Street subway station Dave turned and yelled, "D to the fourth power, baby."

"What?" I said.

"Dave & Dave, Dine & Dash." I laughed all the way to my apartment.

"Victory Café, Oakley, Victory Café!" Dave shouted into the phone, which snapped me back from thinking about last night.

"We dined and dashed, remember?"

"Yeah, but how would he know that?"

"We were wearing our Y&R softball jerseys." I was speechless. The scene of Dave and me jumping up and running out of the restaurant flashed through my mind again. I had totally forgotten what we were wearing.

"Oh fuck…" I muttered into the phone. I looked at my watch and it was 8:55. "I'll meet you in the elevator bank on the fourteenth floor in three minutes."

The fourteenth floor was the executive floor at Y&R. I had never been there. I was just a lowly junior copywriter who a mere five minutes earlier had convinced himself that he was on the fast track at the world's largest ad agency. Now the worldwide chairman wanted to see us. It was like going to the principal's office. Only worse. The elevator door opened and Dave stepped out. He was wearing a white button-down shirt and nice jeans. He looked pretty together for someone who had been completely buzzed a mere seven hours earlier.

We walked over to Mr. Knob's secretary's desk. "Are you boys the ones on the softball team?" she asked. We nodded. "Mr. Knob is not too happy with you." She walked over to his office and knocked on the door and opened it slightly. "Mr. Knob, Mr. Shih and Mr. Oakley are here to see you."

We heard him say, "Send them in."

The secretary turned back toward Dave and me and said, "He'll see you now." As we passed, she whispered, "Thanks for pissing in his corn flakes this morning."

Brian Knob's office was like nothing I had ever seen before in real life. The walls were dark mahogany with oil painting portraits of Y&R's founders. There was a black-and-white photograph of a pro football player, the kind who played without a facemask. From a dark corner of this cavernous room a voice called out. "Do you know who that is?"

"Yes, that's Raymond Rubicam and John Young, Y&R's founders," I responded, amazed at my body's ability to remember their names at the same time as preventing a massive diarrhea attack.

"That's right. But I was asking about the football player." I had no clue, and Dave took a guess.

"George Halas?"

Mr. Knob laughed and said, "No, that's me."

"Wow, you played pro football?"

"Yes, I did," he said as he stood up from behind his desk, revealing his hulking six foot six frame. "I played for the New York Titans. When I was on that team, wherever I went, I was representing the Titans. My actions were always a reflection of that team. When you wear a city's name across your chest you are expected to make the city proud. And when you wear a company's name across your chest the same is expected of you. Especially if that company is Young & Rubicam, the greatest advertising agency in the world," he bellowed at us. "Do you know what I'm talking about?"

Dave and I just sat there. Almost afraid to breathe. "Every morning I arrive at 285 Madison at seven o'clock. I read the *Wall Street Journal* and the ad trades. I call clients and check in with our offices around the world. Do you know what I was doing at seven o'clock this morning?" We both shook our heads. "I took a call from Ned Yost. Do you know Ned Yost? Of course you don't," he answered before we had a chance. "Ned Yost is the owner of the Victory Café, who happens to be a close personal friend of mine."

Oh shit, I thought.

"Ned told me that early this morning two guys wearing Y&R

softball jerseys ran out of his establishment without paying. I said to him that that was impossible. Young & Rubicam does not employ thieves. He insisted that it happened and he said that the two men were wearing number 12 and number 00. I thanked him for calling and told him that I would get to the bottom of it. I asked that for the time being that he not involve the police."

Then he stared at me for about five hours, which probably was only really five seconds, and then turned his gaze to Dave. "So Ken Kadet tells me that you are number 12 and number 00. Is that correct?" I looked at Dave and Dave looked at me.

"I'm number 12," Dave said, meek as a lamb.

"OK," said Mr. Knob, "and you, sir, must be number 00."

I swallowed hard and said, "Yes, I am."

"And were you in the Victory Café at one thirty this morning?"

"Uh-huh," we both said at the same time.

"Did you have dinner there?"

"No, we had a late night snack and a couple of beers," I replied.

"We only had one beer each and the waiter never brought us a check," Dave blurted out.

"So you never got a bill, so you figured you didn't have to pay?" Mr. Knob asked.

Then a look came over Dave's face like he had the idea of the century. I swear I saw a light bulb illuminate over his head. "Mr. Knob, we send our clients monthly bills for our services right?"

"Yes."

"So what if one month we forgot to send a bill to Rolaids? Do you think they would automatically send us our money?"

"Probably not," replied Mr. Knob.

"The waiter was giving us terrible service and then he never brought the bill. We couldn't be expected to pay."

"I see where you're going, Mr. Shih, but your theory is flawed.

First of all, Y&R never gives a client terrible service. And if we ever forgot to send a bill, we'd just send them a reminder that they owed us. Plus interest. And that's what Ned from Victory Café did by calling me. He reminded me that Y&R had forgotten to pay our bill. You know what that means? It means that the two of you'd better be back at Victory Café by the close of business today to pay your bill... if you have any interest at all in keeping your jobs at Y&R. And you'd better leave a really large tip. Now get outta here."

"I'm really sorry Mr.—" I mumbled.

"Get out," he interrupted. As we both got up and shuffled toward the door he continued, "You have disgraced your jersey. And more importantly you have disgraced Young & Rubicam." I was never so happy to get to the door of a room in my life. As I turned the doorknob Mr. Knob bellowed, "Wait. Get over here." I looked back and he was standing beside the paintings of Raymond Rubicam and John Young.

"Apologize to the founders of this company."

"What?" Dave and I said at the same time.

"You heard me. Tell Raymond and John you're sorry."

"Are you serious?" Dave said.

"As serious as I am about firing you if you don't." Dave and I looked at each other and then up to Mr. Knob. Then we faced the founders. When I moved from North Carolina to New York I figured I'd do new things. But never did I think talking to an oil painting would be one of them.

"Apologize," said Mr. Knob.

"I'm sorry, Mr. Rubicam. I'm sorry, Mr. Young," we said in unison. I'm not sure whether or not they accepted our apologies. They just stood there, expressionless, saying nothing. It was a quiet moment that was shattered by Mr. Knob sternly saying, "Now get the fuck out of my office."

This time we got out of there. We went straight to Victory Café and paid them double what the bill was. We kept our jobs. But I learned a valuable lesson: I never dined and dashed wearing a softball jersey again.

YOUR EYES NEVER AGE

DID YOU EVER NOTICE THAT ABOUT 98 PERCENT OF ACTORS AND ACTRESSES IN COMMERCIALS ARE EXTREMELY FIT AND GOOD-LOOKING? It's a not-so-secret secret of advertising. Sex sells. Men enjoy looking at attractive women. Women enjoy looking at attractive men. We all enjoy looking at attractive people. It's a natural phenomenon.

I was thinking about this the other day, as I was registering a domain name with Go Daddy. Was I going with Godaddy.com versus Register.com because of their provocative advertising? Not consciously, but maybe. I wondered, does the fact that I occasionally check out women half my age make me a dirty old man (or a dirty middle-aged man)? No, it just makes me a man. Men enjoy looking at women.

I notice women who are half my age, women who are my age, and even women twice my age. Truthfully, I've never seen a 100-year-old who really got me going, but when Claire's that age, I'm sure she will still be turning heads. I can say with the utmost confidence that some man will be checking her out.

Why am I so sure about this? Because Arnie Arlow told me so. Arnie was my creative director at TBWA back in the early 1990s. Arnie was a stylish fifty-seven-year-old man with impeccable taste in clothes.

He wore Armani suits and called me strange words that this country boy had not heard before, words like *meshugenah*. We hit it off immediately. I think it was because he had never met anyone from the South before and thought I was some sort of oddity. For some reason, he always called me Robert Redford. I did have my hair cut in kind of a *Great Gatsby* style then, and I was blond, but believe me, I didn't look like Robert Redford. For a while, I thought maybe his eyesight was failing, but I later found that not to be the case.

At TBWA, at least half the agency was Jewish, so we got all the Jewish holidays off, which was awesome. I sure wouldn't have gotten those days off if I had taken a job in Raleigh. On the morning of Rosh Hashanah, Arnie was standing in the hallway with Feldman, Lubalin, and Dailey as I walked toward my office. Arnie said to me as I passed, "Hey, Redford, you headed to temple tonight?" I stopped, turned to the fellows and said, without missing a beat, "Of course, Arnie."

"Really? What temple?"

"I'm worshiping at the Temple Beth Rosenblum tonight."

Beth Rosenblum was an account coordinator at TBWA. She was also smoking hot. Arnie howled with laughter.

"Did you hear that?" he said. "Redford's worshiping at the Temple Beth Rosenblum."

The rest of the afternoon, I heard Arnie repeat, "Did you hear what temple Redford is worshiping at tonight?" five more times.

If you asked Arnie today to name one piece of advertising that I produced in my four years at TBWA, he wouldn't be able to name a single thing. But he could tell you what temple I was worshiping at for Rosh Hashanah 1992.

A couple of weeks later, I was walking with Arnie along Madison Avenue. As we passed the Au Bon Pain French bakery on the corner of 41st Street, a very attractive brunette in her early twenties walked past. She was a head-turner. We both smiled at her as she confidently strode by.

"Arnie, did you see her?" I said.

He just said, "Wow."

"Wow is right," I said.

He said, "I saw her. She was gorgeous. But she didn't see me. She saw you. She was smiling right at you."

I thought he was just joking and I said, "No, she was checking you out."

"No, David, she didn't even notice me. What she saw was a nice-looking young man walking with an older gentleman."

"But you noticed her, right?" I asked, halfway wondering if Arnie wasn't interested in the ladies. Then he dropped the bomb.

"The thing that happens as you get older, David, is that your body ages. Your muscles aren't as tight. Your hair turns gray. Your skin wrinkles. But one part of your body never ages."

"Let me guess," I said. "Your johnson?"

"No believe me, that ages." He chuckled and pointed to his eyes and said, "But your eyes…your eyes, David…they never age."

"What the hell are you talking about?"

"You see, I looked at that young lady the same way I would have looked at her when I was twenty. She looked back and saw a fifty-seven-year-old man. I may have a fifty-seven-year-old body but I still have twenty-year-old eyes. And they'll always be twenty. A man will always see the world through the eyes of a twenty-year-old. No matter how old he gets."

I looked at him like he was crazy. But as the years have passed, I realize that Arnie could not have been more correct. Men's eyes never age. Just yesterday, I found myself admiring a voluptuous twenty-five-year-old at the Harris Teeter and I thought of Arnie. I heard his voice saying, "Don't feel guilty, David. Your twenty-year-old eyes are checking out an older woman."

ARE YOU SERIOUS?

A **GREAT SALES JOB TAKES PLANNING.** Especially if the product you're selling is yourself. Proposing to Claire certainly was no exception. In fact, convincing Claire's parents it was a good idea for their daughter to marry a guy from Creedmoor who had no money was the best sales job I've ever pulled off.

People get engaged every day. In fact, I just read that over two million people get married every year in the United States. If I had known then that it was so easy to get hitched, maybe I wouldn't have come up with such an elaborate plan to convince them that I was the right guy for their daughter.

But at the time, I didn't know. So I went all out. And I learned something that has really helped me in my ad career: It takes meticulous planning to be spontaneous.

"IT TAKES METICULOUS PLANNING TO BE SPONTANEOUS.

I had a three-part plan. The first part of my plan was to decide that I wanted to marry Claire. Unlike every other decision in my life, this was an easy one. I didn't waffle one bit. I knew she was the one. The next part of my plan was to ask her father's permission. Then, I was going to propose to Claire. Simple plan. But I wanted to do it in a way that would be endearing, surprising, and unforgettable. And of course, result in a "Yes."

Asking Claire's father Joe's permission to marry her was probably going to be the toughest to pull off. Claire was the youngest of four daughters and the older sisters were all married. And each of the brothers-in-law had asked for Joe's blessing to marry his daughter. I thought this was very respectful, but it was kind of old-school. Why should I only get Joe's permission? Didn't Claire's mom Pam raise her too? I decided to ask both of them at the same time. That way, I figured the odds were less that I'd be denied. More than likely it would be a split decision. Joe would say, "Forget about it," and Pam would say "Of course!" And then the two of them would get in a big fight about it, and eventually Pam would convince Joe to let me marry Claire.

At least that's what I was thinking when I made the call to invite them to dinner. I asked them to come into Manhattan to have a surprise meal with Claire. I explained to them that I wanted to surprise Claire because she had been working really hard and needed a nice break. They loved the idea, and agreed to keep it quiet and meet us at Nanni Il Valletto Thursday evening at seven thirty.

A year earlier, when I first met Claire's dad Joe, he reminded me a lot of Robert De Niro's character in *Meet the Parents*. Actually, he was more like the Robert De Niro character in *The Godfather*. He was a tough, sharp-dressed, self-made, Italian-American man who wore a pinkie ring, which in my mind immediately connected him to the mob. To say he was intimidating would be a gross understatement. I may have been from North Carolina, but I had seen what Michael Corleone was capable of.

The *Meet the Parents* similarity is actually only because I felt like I was meeting him for the first time every time I went over to their house. He had a way of making me feel welcome, yet totally uncomfortable. Every time I visited, he would ask me where I was going with my career. I would stumble through some lame answer about how I would like to become a really respected copywriter and win some

One Show Pencils, and by the time I had finished he was deep into reading the *Wall Street Journal* and wasn't even listening to me. Why should he? He probably figured that every time he saw me would be the last time. There was no way his daughter was going to marry a hillbilly from North Carolina.

Claire's mom, Pam, was a different story. We immediately liked each other. We met for the first time at a Sunday brunch at the Radisson Hotel in Rye. As we stood in the buffet line, the first words she spoke to me were, "What are you having for brunch, David? You look like a beef man to me."

"Yes, I am a beef man," I replied. "I love a good steak."

"So do I, Dave. We probably have a lot in common." Pam replied. She didn't look like she ate a lot of beef. Pam was beautiful. She might have been sixty years old at the time, but she was a head-turner. I was convinced that if Claire looked half as good at sixty as Pam did, I'd be the luckiest man alive.

I arrived at the restaurant at seven twenty, and Pam and Joe were already seated.

"Where's Claire?" Joe said to me as I joined them at the table.

"Oh, she's running late and asked me to meet her here," I replied. This was totally believable because Claire has never been on time for anything in her life. In fact, she was twenty minutes late for our wedding.

"That's great," Pam said. "It'll give us some time to spend with you. Would you like a glass of cabernet?"

"Thank you," I said, knowing that I'd need a couple of glasses to muster my courage.

"So what's going on in the big advertising career these days, David?" Joe asked, as usual. I yammered on about working on the Rolaids account, and gulped down my wine. Every forty-five seconds or so, Joe would glance at his watch.

They asked how my parents were doing, what the weather was like in North Carolina in January, and whether the Giants had a chance in the playoffs. Joe looked at his watch for the twentieth time and said, "Where is she?"

"Honey, you know Claire," Pam responded and poured me another glass of wine.

Joe fidgeted in his chair as our conversation turned to the color of the drapes in the restaurant. As it became clear that we were running out of things to talk about, Joe became increasingly annoyed at Claire's tardiness. "For God's sake, this girl will be late for her own funeral," he blurted out.

"Just relax, Joe," Pam said to him.

"Don't tell me to relax, Pam. Where the hell is our daughter?" For a moment, I thought he was going to leave and go looking for her.

That's when I knew it was time for me to talk. Time for me to make the sales pitch of my life. I had to convince him that a life with me would be the best thing for his baby girl. I took a deep breath and said, "Claire won't be joining us for dinner tonight."

"Why not?" Joe asked quickly.

"Well…" I paused to collect myself. "I didn't invite her."

"What?" Joe asked incredulously, as Pam started to smile. She knew then what was going on.

"I didn't invite her for a reason. I wanted the three of us to have dinner together, so I could ask your permission to marry Claire. I'm in love with her and want to spend the rest of my life with her." Joe sank back in his chair with a slight grin and a sparkle in his eye.

"Oh, David!" Pam exclaimed.

"That is fantastic. Just fantastic. Let's raise a glass to the newest member of our family," Joe said, and he toasted me. Then he got up and hugged me. Then I hugged Pam. Joe called the waiter over and ordered two more bottles of wine. Although Joe's mood had done a

180 in a matter of seconds, I still wasn't sure whether he was celebrating or drowning his sorrows. We stayed at the restaurant until almost eleven, telling stories about Claire and getting hammered together.

The highlight of the evening (after them saying yes) was some information that Pam shared with me.

"There's something about Claire that you should know," Pam said as she reached across the table and held my hand. She looked me square in the eye as if she was going to give me some news that might make me reconsider my thoughts of marrying her. Like maybe she had some kind of rare disease, or something even worse. She patted the top of my hand with her right hand. My left hand was still holding my glass of wine. "David, Claire has been with other boys," she said solemnly.

She waited a few seconds for my reaction. I didn't say anything at first, and then I looked her dead in the eye and said, "Well, now she is marrying a man." I said it with a straight face.

Pam smiled and patted my hand again and said, "Oh, David."

I must say, it was a pretty good quick response on my part. It was all I could do to resist my initial instinct to jokingly say, "She's not a virgin? *Are you kidding me?* Are you gently caressing my hand and saying that your daughter is a slut? A whore? A bed-hopping strumpet?"

I had decided that Claire was the girl of my dreams a few months before. There was a point when I realized that she was the best thing that was ever going to happen to me. And I couldn't and wouldn't live without her. She was tall, she was thin, she was a beautiful brunette, she cussed like Public Enemy, and she made me laugh. Best of all, she liked the NFL even more than I did. The NFL thing is *big*. (Words of advice to my son Lucas and all single guys: if your girlfriend is not a football fan, do not marry her.)

"YOUR MOST IMPORTANT CLIENT IS YOURSELF.

Now that I had talked Pam and Joe into it, I had to win Claire over. She had called me at my apartment and left several messages that evening while I was out with her parents. I called her back as soon as Pam and Joe dropped me off. She wanted me to come over, but I told her that I had decided to hang out with my friends Adam Kandell and Dave Shih instead, and that I'd pick her up the next morning for the drive to Vermont. We were going skiing together. Claire said that I sounded drunk. I was. But nothing compared to how I would be after hanging with Adam and Dave and having them feed me celebratory Wild Turkey shots for the next three hours.

The next morning I felt like I had been run over by a NJ Transit bus. I dragged myself out of bed and stuffed my ski jacket and pants into a duffel bag and took the number 4 train to Grand Central. I walked over to the Avis office on 43rd and rented a Ford Taurus. I'm surprised they rented it to me. I was still wasted. Actually, it had only been five hours since I went to sleep. Luckily, Avis didn't breathalize me.

I drove to pick Claire up at her apartment on 73rd Street. She was waiting in the lobby with her bags. She walked to the car without saying a word. In fact, she didn't say good morning to me until we were almost to Connecticut. She was pissed. *Good*, I thought. *She'll never suspect that I'm about to ask her to marry me.* But even that thought of reassurance didn't comfort my hangover. It was all I could do not to roll the window down and barf onto the Merritt Parkway.

Finally as we were passing Greenwich, she spoke. "What the hell did you do last night?"

"I went out with Dave and Adam. We went to Kinsale Tavern and started doing shots."

"What was the occasion?"

"It was Thursday."

This answer was met with another hour of silence.

We finally arrived at Mount Snow about five in the afternoon. We checked into our bed and breakfast, had a glass of wine that I could barely drink, and went out to dinner. I was feeling a little better by then and Claire was psyched to be back in Vermont. Claire was really looking forward to a full day of skiing the next day. We vowed to be on the slopes early.

While Claire was brushing her teeth, I went over my plan again in my head. I would propose to Claire on the last run of the day. I knew that once I popped the question, we'd be too excited to ski. I wanted to get my money's worth. (After all, the lift tickets were $59 each.) Then I stuffed all of my extra gear for the occasion into my ski jacket: a bottle of champagne, two champagne glasses, a corkscrew, (even though I realized later that you don't need a corkscrew to open a bottle of champagne) a camera, and a beautiful diamond-and-sapphire engagement ring. This loot made my ski jacket an extremely snug fit.

As we went up the chairlift for the first run of the day, I started getting nervous. What if she didn't say yes? How embarrassing would that be? I thought about it for a minute and considered an even worse outcome: *What if I wipe out before I propose? What if I do one of those thrill-of-victory-agony-of-defeat faceplants?* I've done a couple of them before, but not when I had a bottle of champagne strapped across my chest. If I fell on that bottle it would either break my ribs or the bottle would break and slice my chest open. When I skied off the top of the lift, I was extremely cautious.

We skied a couple of blue intermediate runs to warm up, and I almost busted my ass three times. Each time, Claire was at the bottom of the run a good minute before I got there. On our third run, we decided to try a black expert run. By this time, I was so nervous that I knew that I would never make it to the last run of the day. I almost fell getting off the chairlift, so I decided that this would be THE run.

We skied about halfway down and I went over to the side and stopped for a moment. I told Claire that there was something in my boot. She was slightly annoyed that I was slowing down her shredding. I took my boot completely off and started to get down on one knee when two women in their sixties skied up and stopped right beside us.

"Lovely day, isn't it?" one of the ladies said to Claire.

"Yes it is," she responded. Claire looked back over at me and said, "What are you doing?"

"There's a rock in my ski boot," I said, wishing to myself that those ladies would get the hell out of there. Finally, they skied away. I again started to get down on one knee. I unbuckled my other boot for a little more flexibility and no kidding, a couple of ski patrol dudes quickly skied up beside up with a sled behind one of them.

"There he is," one said to the other.

"Are you OK?" the other one said to me.

"He's fine. He's got a rock in his boot and several in his head. He's OK," said my impatient wife-to-be.

"Well, we got a radio call that there was someone injured on this run."

"It's not me. I'm just fixing my boot," I said.

The two of them stayed beside us, talking for what seemed like an hour. I'm sure it was no more than two or three minutes, but it took forever for them to leave. As soon as they skied away, I kicked my second boot off and quickly got down on one knee.

"Claire, I love you and want to spend the rest of my life with you. I want you to be my wife. Will you marry me?" Claire looked at me in stunned silence for several seconds, and then fell back into the snow bank.

"Are you serious?" she said with a giant smile.

"You're damn right I'm serious!" I reached into my pocket and fumbled around looking for the ring box, thinking that every time I've ever seen a proposal in the movies, the girl immediately says yes. She doesn't question whether you are serious or not. Men don't joke around about this shit. If you ask someone to marry you, you are serious or you are seriously out of your mind—or both. Or maybe she was asking, "Are you serious?" because I am always joking around and playing practical jokes on people and she just knows me really well.

I finally found the ring box and pulled it out. I opened it and showed the ring to her. "So…will you marry me?" I asked.

"Yes, yes, yes," she replied, as she got out of the snow and jumped on me. I slid the engagement ring on her finger.

"Did you talk with my father about it?"

"Yes I did. And I talked with your mom about it too. And they both said yes."

"When did you talk with them?"

"Thursday night."

"Oh my God, oh my God, oh my God."

"And boy, do your parents like their red wine. That's why I was so hungover yesterday."

"Oh wait, I almost forgot." I reached into my jacket and pulled out the bottle of champagne and the glasses. I popped the cork and poured us each a glass. We raised our glasses and toasted each other and our future together. I reached back into my pocket and felt something I had totally forgotten about. My disposable camera. I reached my left arm around and snapped our first engaged photo together.

I pulled it off. It was a sales job of a lifetime.

The moment she said yes, I thought the pitch was over. But I was wrong. It was just the beginning. I've been selling Claire on me every day since. And after she reads this book, I have a feeling I'm going to have a lot more selling to do.

She said yes.

SNEEZING ON SYDNEY

I LOVED LIVING IN NEW YORK CITY. My eight years there were some of the best times of my life. I met my wife there. I produced my first ad there. I had an office on Madison Avenue. I went to plays. I went to Yankees games, Giants games, and Rangers games. I saw MC Hammer host *Saturday Night Live*. I ate the best food in the world.

And I did it all on a junior copywriter's salary.

But there came a time when I wanted more. I wanted more freedom to create. I wanted to be away from the bureaucracy of a behemoth agency. I didn't enjoy the layers upon layers of approvals for my work that came with working at a 1,400-person shop. I have always felt I was more of a "make-it-happen" guy, rather than a person who worked in theory and process. I guess that's why I get so much enjoyment out of mowing grass, because you can immediately see the work that you have done, instead of waiting for months to find out if your work is produced. Plus I really missed North Carolina. I wanted a yard to mow.

That being said, I probably would still be in a New York agency if not for one incident—an incident that had absolutely nothing to do with advertising.

Claire and I were living in a tiny apartment right off Union Square, just below 14th Street. Three months earlier, our daughter Sydney had been born. We were typical overprotective first-time parents. One Sunday morning, the three of us were going to go out for a stroll around the neighborhood. We bundled up and strapped

Sydney into her stroller/baby carrier and went to wait for the elevator.

The door opened on the twelfth floor and we got in. The elevator stopped on the third floor. As the doors opened, a man sneezed loudly and blew his nose into a tissue. Then he walked into the elevator. "God bless you," Claire said to him, politely.

He wiped his nose and stuffed the tissue into his pocket, and with the same hand that seconds earlier had been covered with snot, reached down and rubbed Sydney's face. "What a beautiful little baby," he said to Claire, as he breathed in heartily to keep the snot from his nose from running down over his lip. The doors on the elevator opened and the man turned and walked into the lobby before we could even say anything to him. He just rubbed his germs on Sydney's face and left us standing there with our mouths agape.

That afternoon, Sydney started sneezing. She had her first cold. Her nose started running that evening (and has been perpetually running ever since).

After spending a sleepless night with a miserable baby fighting a terrible cold, we made a decision. It was time to give up the Yankees, the restaurants, and the Madison Avenue office for some more space. The next morning, I called a recruiter and told him that I was ready to leave New York. Two months later, we moved to Charlotte. Now we've been here for twenty years. It was the best move ever. For my family. And my career.

I wish I knew that guy in the elevator's name. I'd really like to send him a thank-you note.

But before I send it, I'm going to let Sydney blow her nose into the envelope.

GRAVEL IN THE DRIVEWAY

Three years after we left New York, Claire and I were living in Charlotte. We were now a family of four, as our son Lucas had been born six months earlier.

FELT A LITTLE FUNNY AFTER MY FIFTH DRINK THAT AFTERNOON. I should have known better than to down almost a whole pitcher by myself, but it really wasn't that unusual. I did it two or three times a week.

I'm not talking about rum punches or kamikazes, my friend. I'm talking about a pitcher of true southern discomfort, the Charlotte ad man's drink of choice in 1997: none other than sweet tea. Whenever I needed to concentrate on coming up with ideas, I'd sit and sip iced tea with my art director all day long. A caffeine buzz more often than not led me to some pretty memorable ads. On this day, it led me to the most unforgettable pain I've ever experienced.

Around four o'clock, after swilling Lipton since noon, I said to my art director Michael Cohen that we should head back to the agency. He agreed, and we paid our tab at the Tyber Creek Pub and headed out into the wonderful mid-February Charlotte weather: thirty-eight degrees and pissing rain. We ran over to his silver Mazda RX-7 and hopped in. We had driven all of two blocks when I felt a sharp twinge in my lower back. I yelled at Michael to stop the car. He looked at me like I had completely lost my mind and said, "What?"

"Stop the car. I gotta get out. I can't sit anymore." I opened the door before he came to the stoplight and jumped out. I ran out into the near-freezing rain and grabbed my knees and just stood there, dealing with what felt like someone jabbing me in my back with a butcher knife. The pain subsided after a couple of minutes and I realized that I was getting soaked. So I walked over to an awning on the side of Zarelli's Restaurant to get a bit of shelter.

Michael drove around and rolled down his window. "What the hell? Are you OK?" I responded that this was very weird as I got back into his car and we drove back to the agency. We made it back to Price McNabb, which was by far the best ad agency in the NationsBank tower. (Considering it was the only agency in a building that primarily housed bankers and lawyers, you can draw your own conclusions.)

Just before I got back to my office, the full force of the pain hit me again. And I mean it hit me so hard it knocked me straight to the floor. Right in front of agency president Norm Green's office. "Motherfucker. Motherfucker. Motherfucker," I cried in agony. Norm jumped out of his seat and immediately came out of his office. I guess he thought I was calling him. In a rare compassionate moment, he asked, "Dave, are you OK?"

"Motherfucker. Motherfucker," I replied. Then I barfed an iced tea and tuna melt combo right on his Bruno Maglis. Come to think of it, I never saw him wear them again. After I spewed, I felt better again, but I knew something was seriously wrong.

Michael asked if I had a personal physician. I said yes and I gave Dr. Sam a call. When I think back on this, it's hard to believe that I called Dr. Sam and he actually took my call. I described my symptoms and he knew exactly what it was. "David," he said, "you have a kidney stone. I'm going to call you in a prescription of Valium and you should go directly to the pharmacy and take two. And you should flush your kidneys. Drink as much water as possible and maybe, just maybe, you will be able to pass the stone. Either way, come see me on Monday."

"Wait a minute," I said, "I'm going to pass the stone?"

"Yes, David, it will pass through your urethra."

"What the hell is my ethra?"

"Your urethra is…"

"Your your ethra? Why are you stuttering, Dr. Sam? I'm the one that's about to pass a rock thru my penis!"

Dr. Sam remained composed and clinical and he said, "The urethra, U-R-E-T-H-R-A, is the tube that carries liquid wastes out of your body in the form of urine. The kidney stone will pass through your urethra, which is in your penis."

"So I'm going to piss out a rock?"

"It's not a rock, it's a very, very small calcium deposit."

"If it's so freaking small why does it hurt so much?" I moaned.

"The stone is tiny, but it is calcified, which means it has hardened with razor-sharp hooks and spikes protruding from it, which grab and stab the surfaces that it passes through. That's why you were in such pain. The stone is likely passing from your kidney into your bladder. The next logical step is for it to pass through your urethra."

I don't know about you, but the thought of razor sharp hooks and spikes slicing their way through my johnson were not the words of comfort I was looking for. "So what am I supposed to do?" I asked.

"As I said, flush your kidneys, take two Valium, and hopefully it will pass naturally. And I'd like you to schedule an appointment to see me on Monday morning, whether you pass it or not."

"What do you mean if I don't pass it?"

"It may be too big to pass, in which case we'll use our ultrasound machine to break it up."

I didn't hear any of the second half of his sentence. All I heard was the possibility that it might be too big to pass. All I could imagine was this tiny stone that was actually much bigger than expected getting stuck halfway down my dick. And then it staying there until our office visit on Monday morning. That's when I threw up the second time, splattering my stylish footwear of choice, white Chuck Taylors.

Michael volunteered to drive me home and I took him up on his offer without hesitation. It was about five fifteen and every banker and attorney was leaving downtown. So we joined the parade of BMWs and big SUVs. We had barely made it six blocks when the pain started again. I wasn't about to jump out in the rain again, but I had to do something. I couldn't sit in the seat anymore. So I leaned my seat back, turned around, and got on my hands and knees with my head in the backseat and my ass facing forward. It was the only way I could position myself that made the pain in my back halfway bearable.

"Get me to the drug store now. This fucking hurts, motherfucker." I don't normally cuss indiscriminately, but something about this brought out the sailor in me. I only recall a couple of things clearly from the drive to get my drugs.

One, Michael was really calm and said, "I've heard that having a kidney stone is the closest thing to the pain of childbirth."

I replied, "Women are some tough motherfuckers. Cause this is kicking my ass."

The second thing I remember is that we got stopped at a railroad crossing by a freight train. I have never before or since been stopped by a train in Charlotte. But one stopped us when I was in labor about to give birth to a chunk of gravel.

Valium is a wonder drug. As soon as the pharmacist handed me the prescription, I downed two pills chased by a bottle of Dasani. Within minutes, my pain was a distant memory. I felt fantastic. Thank goodness I had Michael to drive me home. When I arrived at Casa Oakley, I was a new man. Claire had been home with the kids all day and, as it so often happens when you have a six-month-old and a three-year-old, she was exhausted. She asked how I was feeling and I told her much better. So much better, in fact, that I felt inclined to put on some Stevie Wonder and dance around the living room while we made dinner. I was enjoying my new pal Val.

But I hadn't forgotten the doctor's orders: flush my kidneys. So I continued to drink water. And drink water. And drink more water. By the time we put the kids to bed, I had consumed a whole gallon of water. I hadn't even gotten the slightest urge to go to the bathroom. It's no wonder. I knew that whatever passed from my kidney to my bladder was going to have to pass through my whatever it was that Dr. Sam called it.

Finally the urge to pee was greater than my fear of the great spiky boulder slicing and dicing me from the inside out. So with great trepidation, I walked into the bathroom. I stood in front of the toilet and slid my jeans down to my knees. I leaned forward and braced myself by putting both hands against the wall. I said a little prayer and opened the dam.

The piss started flowing like Old Milwaukee on spring break. I kept myself braced against the wall. And the river kept on flowing. Then suddenly, the flow stopped. Any guy who's reading this knows that a flow like this never just stops. But it stopped. For a split second. And when it started again, the first thing I saw was what looked like a black bb shooting into the toilet. Thank God I was braced against the wall because I nearly fainted. Not from the pain, but from the sheer size of it. It was a similar reaction that some people have when they see their own blood. Like, "Fuck! That came out of me?" The spiky bb hit the bottom of the toilet with so much force that it nearly cracked the bowl. The "bing" that it made upon impact was so loud that our dog started barking. I peed for what seemed like another twenty minutes. Finally I finished, but I still had a major task at hand. I had to retrieve the stone from the toilet. It might gross some people out that I simply reached through the pee and grabbed the stone, but after what I had just been through, sticking my hand in a bowl of piss was not a problem. I rinsed the spiky specimen off and put it in a ziplock bag to take to Dr. Sam.

The next day was a big day if you worked at an ad agency in Charlotte. It was the annual Charlotte ADDYs, where the best ads of the year are recognized. I really wanted to go, since some of my work was nominated for awards, but after having passed a kidney stone, I wasn't so sure I was up for it. When I walked outside midafternoon to check the mail, I noticed something that made me realize that I was definitely going. I picked up a piece of gravel in the driveway with a plan in mind...

Claire and I got dressed and headed to downtown Charlotte that evening. When we got to the ADDYs everyone was glad to see us and very happy to hear that I was feeling better. The ADDYs are one of those parties where everyone gets pretty hammered, and this year was no different. Actually there was one difference. I wasn't participating in the revelry. I was just enjoying the pain-free life with a little help from Val.

After our work for Charlotte Plastic Surgery had won best of show, Rene Hodges, my dear friend who was president of the Ad Club at the time, came over and hugged me. "Well, you won again, you little Shitbird." I grinned because she always calls me Shitbird. I love that name. I guess it's kind of like being a high class shitass.

"I think that billboard is your best work ever," she said.

I said, "No, you're wrong, Rene. My best work is right here." And I reached into my pocket and pulled out the ziplock bag. I held it up and said, "This is the best thing I've ever produced."

"Oh my God. You brought your kidney stone?"

"Yep."

"Let me see it. How the hell did you pass that?"

"It wasn't easy."

She handed it over to her daughter Jenn, and Jenn just said, "Jesus!" Before I knew it at least fifty people had taken a good look at the kidney stone.

"It's so big," "No freaking way," and "That must have hurt," were just a few of the comments. Everyone who saw it was amazed. No one questioned whether it was real or not. Maybe it was because they were drunk. Maybe it was just because no one had ever seen a kidney stone before. Certainly no one had brought one to the Charlotte ADDYs before.

And neither did I. I brought the piece of gravel that I found in the driveway.

Which proves the old saying. There's no truth in advertising. And for sure there's no truth at the ADDYs.

TAKING CREDIT

NOTE: The names in this story have been changed to protect the innocent. (Actually, they were changed to keep me from getting sued.)

I HEARD A QUOTE FROM MAYA ANGELOU THE OTHER DAY: "WHEN SOMEONE SHOWS YOU WHO THEY ARE, BELIEVE THEM." These profound words immediately took me back to one of the most bizarre episodes of attempted credit stealing in the history of advertising. OK, maybe not in the history of advertising, but I still can't believe it happened.

It was the mid 1990s and I was hanging out by the fax machine at Charles/Donovan. That's what award-obsessed ad guys like me did in the late '90s: you hung out by the fax machine. Especially in early September. That's when notifications from *Communications Arts* magazine were normally due to come, letting you know whether or not your work had been selected for the prestigious *CA Advertising Annual.*

I heard the whirr of the machine. The green Transmit button lit up. A fax was coming through. I stared in amazement as out rolled two faxes from *CA.*

The first fax said that our TV commercial for a paper company got into the annual. The second fax said that a print ad that we'd done for a real estate development company was selected. This was unbelievable. This was awesome news. I ran around the office like a chicken with its head cut off, high-fiving everyone that I saw. I was flipping out.

This was the reason that I'd moved from a large New York agency to work at a small Charlotte shop. Fewer layers and less bureaucracy. It was a place where I could do great work. Great work that would get us in the award annuals. This was one of the best days ever (in advertising). It was proof to me that coming back south was the right move.

I congratulated everyone in the office. Unfortunately, most of the creatives who'd worked on the projects with me were no longer at the agency. Savannah Scott, a copywriter, and Clay Tryon, the creative director on the projects, had left the agency two months earlier. At least Shelly McDougal, the art director, was there. I gave her a big hug and then ran into Rachel Kramer's office and told her. Rachel was the new creative director. We were on top of the world.

Everyone at Charles/Donovan was psyched. This was the best day since, well, since ever.

Later that day, I was sitting in my office still basking in the glow of victory. Rachel Kramer came in with a weird look on her face and said, "We've got a little problem with those ads getting into *CA*."

"Problem? How can there be a problem? This is the best thing that's ever happened to this agency."

"Yeah, there's a problem. I just talked with Tim Sepe"—he was the president of Charles/Donovan—"and he told me that I needed to talk with you about this."

"Why?"

"Because our policy is that we don't mention anyone in any press or publications after they have left the agency."

"What does that mean?" I asked.

"It means that on the credits for the ads that got into *CA*, we will not be able to put Clay Tryon's name on them as creative director."

"But he *was* the creative director," I said

"Yes," Rachel replied, "but Clay doesn't work here anymore. So his name will not be published in *CA*. We don't want our future clients thinking that someone who used to work here did the good work."

"So we're just going to leave the creative director's name blank?"

"No, we'll put my name there, since I'm the creative director now."

"But you weren't the creative director on these ads. It's not the truth."

"Well I'm going to be listed as the creative director of these ads. We don't want to confuse our clients. Present or future."

She turned and left the room. My day had just gone from the best ever to the absolute worst. *How could anyone stoop so low?* I thought. *How could anyone take credit for someone else's ideas?* I'd heard about it before, but I didn't really believe that people did that.

I left the office and immediately called Clay, who had been free-lancing since he'd been let go. At first he was in shock. Then, understandably, he was livid.

He said he was going to call his lawyer. This was a clear violation of his separation agreement. Not giving him credit for these award-winning ads would hinder his future employment opportunities. Clay thanked me for the heads-up and said that he would talk with me later.

The next morning Clay called me before I left for the office. He said that Charles/Donovan would be receiving a fax from his lawyer at nine a.m.

About nine fifteen, I was in a meeting with Rachel and the rest of the creative staff. There was a knock on the door and Lori Mitchell, the head of PR, walked in. She was holding a sheet of paper in her hand. Lori said to Rachel, "Rachel, I need to speak with you for a moment. We just received a very important fax."

I smiled to myself, because I knew that the proverbial shit was about to hit the fan.

A couple of hours later, I was sitting in my office and Rachel walked in. "About that conversation we had yesterday," she said. "Let's forget it ever happened. I thought about it a lot last night, and I just went and spoke with Tim and the partners about it. I convinced them that we should leave Clay's name on the credits."

I smiled and said, "I'm really glad to hear that, Rachel. It's the right thing to do. We'll get something in *CA* again next year. And then your name will be on it as creative director."

She nodded in agreement and left the room.

I knew at that moment I would be leaving the agency soon. And I would never, ever work with her again.

WHY IS YOUR NAME UPSIDE DOWN?

SOMEONE ASKED ME RECENTLY WHY MY NAME IS UPSIDE DOWN ON OUR BUILDING. It wasn't the first time I'd heard the question. So I gave my standard answer: "Because I'm the crazy one, I guess."

That always seems to get a chuckle. But the truth is, the upside down Oakley has become a symbol of how our agency thinks. It's a simple premise: We look at things from a different perspective. When you do this, more often than not, you see things that you normally wouldn't have seen.

I'm asked at least once every day if I know that the name on our building is upside down—sometimes by people who work here.

When we started our agency, John Boone and I debated at length about whether our name should be BooneOakley or OakleyBoone.

This was a very important decision. Think about it. Have you ever heard of Gamble & Proctor? Or Packard-Hewlett? Or Decker & Black? Of course not. They got the order right when they named their companies. If we made a mistake with this, we'd have to live with it forever.

We designed our logo so that on our business cards, it could be either BooneOakley or OakleyBoone. Boone was right side up and Oakley was upside down, or Boone was upside down and Oakley was right side up. It depended on how you were holding it.

Either way, neither was a particularly inspiring choice as initials. BO or OB? Body odor, or a tampon that caused toxic shock syndrome. We even considered combining names to be BooneOakleyOakley-Boone. BOOB. (We've been called much worse.)

This decision had everything to do with ego. The first name of a company is always the one that everyone remembers. So both of us wanted our name first. Since we couldn't come to an agreement, we decided to put it to a vote.

The vote was John's idea. He said, "Let's let the people decide. We'll ask the public to vote on our website."

"That seems fair," I said.

And for the next thirty days visitors to booneoakley.com or oakleyboone.com placed their votes.

Obviously, BooneOakley won. And it was a landslide. I was a little bummed for a while, but I had agreed to put it to a vote. BooneOakley won fair and square.

At least that's what I thought. Until four years ago. That's when Boone finally fessed up. His brother, a computer whiz, had hacked into our site and voted for BooneOakley over 30,000 times.

So I'm really not the crazy one. I'm the stupid one. Stupid enough to fall for John's scheme to get his name first on the building.

But that's OK. No one has ever asked him why his name is right side up.

TEA YA LATER

NOTE: Some of the names in this story have been changed. Some of them have not been changed. Can you guess which ones?

I T WAS THE PERFECT ACCOUNT. Or at least that's what I thought. Red Berry Tea is an iconic, locally owned, regional brand that has been in business for three-quarters of a century. When we won the business, I had high hopes that it was going to be a golden opportunity to do outstanding creative work. The type of work that a brand like this deserves.

It didn't bother me one bit that the account had been with four different agencies in the previous six years. Not a bit. OK, maybe it was a tiny red flag, but not one that we couldn't overcome. Those other agencies were not BooneOakley. We were different. We were so much *better*. Clearly, we would be able to do what we do best: create work that people share and talk about. I couldn't wait to get started.

What ensued over the next six months was the stuff of legends. It was a series of presentations and re-presentations. Do it and do it over. Great campaigns created, great campaigns killed. Because great wasn't good enough for this iconic brand.

Or should I say more specifically, for this insane client. Yes, every account is run by a person. And this one was run by a certified lunatic. Bat-shit crazy. Let's call him Rob.

We should have known we were in for it in our first meeting, when Rob used twenty-seven advertising clichés in one sentence to describe

Red Berry Tea. "To win the hearts and minds of America, we need to kick the tires on innovative concepts that can be the tip of the spear and still be viral in nature, yet consumer-generated, that can activate a passion brand, a love-mark if you will, like Red Berry Tea, that will break through the clutter on a shoestring marketing budget and connect with our fans as they embark on their journey and experience the one-of-a-kind flavor that is unique to Red Berry Tea."

You gotta be kidding me.

BooneOakley writer Mary Gross came up with a musical radio campaign that took mundane everyday tasks and made them into monumental accomplishments to be celebrated with a glass of Red Berry Tea. I really believe this could have been Red Berry Tea's "Real Men of Genius" (the fantastic Bud Light campaign written by Bob Winter at DDB Chicago). But Rob never "got" the campaign. I kept trying to push it forward. I was determined to get it produced. After meeting with Rob on a Friday afternoon, I was convinced I had sold him on the campaign. He smiled, shook my hand and said, "Great work." On Sunday morning, I got an email from Rob saying that he couldn't get to sleep all night, so he got up and wrote radio commercial scripts until seven in the morning. He requested an in-person meeting on Monday to share his thoughts with me.

I've seen a lot of things in this business, but this was a first for me: a sixty-something client sitting across from me in our conference room, showing *me* "how to write product-centric radio that will resonate with our primary target group, the savvy millennial."

I nodded as I thought, *The average millennial is forty years younger than this guy.*

"You see, David," he continued, "you have to be able to mix the product attributes throughout the spot. Make them part of the listener's journey. That way, you're not selling to them, and our fans will invite us to go along on their road trip with them."

"Uh-huh," I uttered.

"Remember *Zoolander*? The movie? Zoolander was the world's most interesting male model. In this radio spot, Red Berry Tea is the world's most interesting beverage. OK, let me get into character."

He extended his thumb and forefingers together to form a rectangle in front of his face. I guess it's the international sign for "Now I'm on camera." He pursed his lips, tilted his head to the side and gazed blankly into my eyes. Then he began.

> *"My name is Ruby. . . . Ruby is my name.*
> *And I am beautiful . . . almost beyond words.*
> *I walk like a runway model yet I can juggle and knot a cherry stem with my tongue."*

OK, this was already uncomfortable. Now it was starting to get creepy.

> *"I am Ruby and I drink Red Berry Tea . . . it is ruby too.*
> *And beautiful like me . . .*
> *only TAST—IER! JUIC—IER! and SMOOTH—IER! SOR—TA!*
> *It tempts me in aisle seven, always aisle seven,*
> *it teases, it drenches me in fizz."*

Drenches me in fizz?! Did he really just say that? Or did he say *jizz*? I couldn't decide whether to start laughing or start running. Frankly, Rob's little charade had me spellbound. It was perverse. It was lurid. It was absolute madness.

> *"That makes me want it morer . . . more.*
> *When it's cold it's hot . . . like me, kinda, but different.*
> *Follow me . . . Ruby, on Red Berry Tea Facebook under Ruby Red Berry Tea. It's not just tea, it's tea-licious!"*

It'd be one thing if Ben Stiller was sitting across from me, his face contorting, his tongue flapping in and out while he gave me a frozen narcissistic stare. Instead it was a creepy, silver-haired, red-faced, pot-bellied sixty-five-year-old. The only part that made sense was that the character's name was Ruby. It matched the shade of his alcohol-enhanced skin.

When Rob finished his performance, he closed his eyes for a moment. When he opened them, he was no longer Rubylander. He was back in full huckster mode. He said, "You see, David, this is the kind of radio that Red Berry needs. Something that can connect with and capture the imagination of our target. This could be the first step in winning the hearts and minds of America. It could be the first step in making us the next great American brand."

Rob was convinced that his tongue flapping, cherry-stem-knitting, breathless, intoxicated Ruby was just the ticket.

What I should have done was escort Rob to the door and called the police. Instead, I said, "You want our agency to produce this radio?"

"No, no, I'm just showing you this as an example of how it *could* be done. Share it with your team. It should inspire them."

"It sure made an impression on me," I responded.

"Well, I'm sure your team can beat it, but if they can't, we can go with this."

With that, he got up and left. And rather than resign the account, I made a horrible mistake: I subjected our agency to two more months of abuse.

I heard the words of the legendary copywriter Luke Sullivan ringing in my ears: *Outlast the idiots, outlast the idiots...* So for the next two months, our team killed itself coming up with new and better ideas. Only to have them second-guessed, picked apart, and shit upon, then covered up with Rob's heart-sickening torrent of mindless clichés and marketing babble.

*OUTLAST THE IDIOTS.

Every day that we worked on the account, we grew more angry, frustrated, and resentful. Agency morale plummeted. Claire, my wife and our director of client services, ranked Rob the worst client she had ever encountered. Eric, the most laid-back designer I've ever met, couldn't stand the guy. Rob was so nasty to our PR director and account executive that he made both of them cry. Then he asked that they be taken off the business. Lucky them. He was pleasant one minute and completely cruel the next. He fancied himself Johnny Appleseed spreading Red Berry throughout the land. What he was, was Johnny Rotten, poisoning our agency from the inside out.

We finally got to the point that we could no longer take the abuse. We decided that we would make one last-ditch effort and show Red Berry Tea the best work we had ever done. Play our game and leave everything on the field. And if Rob and Red Berry Tea didn't like it, they could go screw themselves.

The day before our presentation to Red Berry Tea, I was on the phone with Mike Palma, a recruiter out of Atlanta, who was helping me with a talent search. He asked how things were going with Red Berry Tea.

"Is Rob still the marketing director?"

I said yes.

"Total douchebag."

"You know Rob?" I asked.

"I helped an agency in Atlanta win that account five years ago. Rob never liked any of the work. What he liked was coming to Atlanta and getting hammered at the Cheetah Lounge. He'd show up the next morning all hungover and kill all the work."

I told him about Rob presenting radio to me to show me how it's supposed to be done. He laughed and said, "I've got Rob stories out the ass. He hated the account person that the agency had on his business. He said she was too junior for him. So the agency recruited a great account supervisor from Chicago. She moved her family to Atlanta and 45 days later Rob asked that she be taken off the business."

"Wow," I said. "Same thing here. We were looking for an account supervisor for him as well."

"Total ass. You'd be better off without him."

You would think that this would make me feel better. It did a little, I guess. But what I realized was that I had put the image of the agency in front of the well-being of the agency. I thought it looked good to the outside that we had the Red Berry Tea account, when in fact, it was killing our spirit from the inside. It was a toxic relationship. No amount of money or prestige can ever overcome that. Our motto for fourteen years has been "Do great work for people you like," and instead we were doing work for a brand we loved and a person we couldn't stand. I wish I had talked with Palma seven months earlier.

Before we started BooneOakley, Pat Doody from Wongdoody asked me what was our agency going to be about. I told him it was going to be all about the work and that we were going to be the best creative shop in the Southeast. His reply shocked me. He said we were destined to fail. *Fail? WTF?* I argued, "We want to be like Wongdoody. You guys are the best creative shop in the Northwest."

"I'm flattered, David, but we're not all about the work. Our creative is probably number seven in our top ten most important things. It's all about relationships. If you don't have a strong relationship, a relationship built on trust and mutual respect, no client will ever give you their business. And you have to get their business long before you do any creative work. And if the client doesn't trust you, there's no way he'll buy what you present."

"So what you're saying is that if you don't have a great relationship, you'll never produce great work."

"Exactly."

I thought about Pat's words as we gathered the team together before we left for the meeting. These guys had put their hearts, souls, and countless hours into work that we were about to present. I thanked our team and congratulated them for a job well done.

I told them that if Rob didn't like the work we were about to present, we were going to end the relationship. "We hope they like the work. They should. It's spot-on strategy. It's funny. And it's something that people will want to share. But if they don't like it, we're done." I don't know if they believed me or not. Probably not. Nobody resigns business anymore.

We drove to Berryville. We presented two stellar, well thought-out campaigns. We would have been thrilled to produce either. The presentation was fantastic. Everyone was on. The media plan was awesome. The PR initiatives were super creative. Simply put, we rocked it. We played our game. We gave it our all.

What did we get in return? A dead fish handshake and, "Thanks for coming in and we'll get back to you in a couple of days."

What a great relationship!

The next day Rob called to talk about the work. "Overall, I don't think either campaign has the spark to set the brand free. We're looking for viral. If anything, we should push more in the direction of the second campaign."

This was our cue.

"Rob, we really think that it's best that we end our relationship. It's clear that we don't see eye-to-eye on how and where to take the brand. It's been an interesting seven months, and we believe we will both be better off if you find another partner. We are resigning the business."

Rob was quiet for a moment and said, "I wholeheartedly agree. But here's the difference. Red Berry Tea is ending the relationship. Not you. Consider this your sixty-day notice."

It was a classic you-can't-quit-because-I'm-firing-you moment. It was a thing of beauty and one I'll never forget. A huge sense of relief came over me. We were done with Red Berry.

When we told the team, they cheered. We all raised a glass to celebrate standing up for what we believed in.

And how did we tell the world? With a tweet, of course:

Hey @redberrytea So you don't think we have the "spark" to help your brand go viral? See how this works: We resign! @adweek @ adage

The twitterverse lit up. *Adweek, Ad Age, Creativity,* and *Media Daily* all posted stories of our resignation within the hour. We had given Red Berry Tea exactly what they wanted: they had gone viral.

OK, OK, we didn't do that. But we thought about it.

Pat Doody was right. In this business, it's all about relationships. And no matter how bad the relationship was, or how bitter the ending, there's really no use in immediately skewering someone in the press.

I think it's much better to wait a while and put it in a book.

WHAT A DIFFERENCE A LOGO MAKES

VISITED SOUTH PARK MALL IN CHARLOTTE RECENTLY TO BUY A COLLARED SHIRT. I went straight to the men's department at Belk and found a nice black Polo shirt. Well, it was nice until I saw the price: $95.

I thought that was kind of steep, so I decided to look for some other options. I found a black shirt that looked exactly like the Polo shirt. The only difference was it didn't have a Polo logo on it. Oh wait, there was another difference: the plain black shirt was only $20.

It's the power of branding. People are happy to pay extra for name-brand logos on their clothes. In this case, a little red man riding a little red horse adds $75 to the price of a plain cotton shirt.

This guy riding a pony adds about $75 in value to everything it touches.

None of this is really news. So why am I writing about it? Because last night I wore my logo-less black shirt to a neighborhood pool party. There I saw quite a few guys wearing Polo shirts. But one stood out so much I had to take a picture.

This Polo shirt must have had over a hundred stitched Polo logos on it. It was like nothing I had ever seen. Claire declared that it must be part of "The Herd" collection. This made me laugh. Hard.

Then I thought, *I wonder how much this guy paid for his shirt?* So I did a little calculation in my head. A hundred Polo logos at $75 each. That's $7500. Plus $20 for the shirt. $7520.

That dude was wearing the world's most expensive shirt.

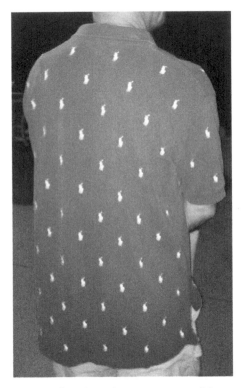

When I die, please bury me in one of these.

WINNING 100 GRAND

WINNING AT ADVERTISING INDUSTRY AWARD SHOWS IS MOSTLY ABOUT BRAGGING RIGHTS. It's about being recognized by your peers as having done the best work of the year. There's really no big financial gain for you in winning a Clio statue or a National ADDY. A Gold One Show Pencil is actually made of brass and has no real value, except maybe as a doorstop or a very dangerous sex toy. Now, the *prestige* that comes from winning a Pencil or a Cannes Lion does have a monetary benefit. The honor makes you much more marketable, and significantly raises the chances that some company will pay you much more than you are actually worth to join them.

Award shows would be so much better if they all gave cash prizes to the winners.

The Outdoor Advertising Association of America sponsors the OBIE Awards every year. The OBIEs honor the best billboards and out-of-home ads every year with a swanky ceremony in New York. The OBIE Awards aren't the most prestigious awards show in the world, but they are my favorite, for two reasons: 1) I love outdoor advertising, and 2) Every year they give $100,000 to their Best of Show winner. That's why we enter the OBIEs every year.

In 2002, we were notified that several of our billboards were selected as finalists. We got a call from Stephen Freitas, the chairman of the OBIEs, who told us that it would be a good idea if we attended the show. When you get a call from an awards show telling you that it would be "a good idea" if you attended, it usually means you won something. They want the winners to be there to walk up on stage to accept their OBIEs. They also want the winner of Best of Show to be there to accept the oversize Publishers Clearing House–style check for $100,000.

As soon as we got the call, I started thinking about winning the 100 Gs. A couple of days later, Gale Bonnell from Adams Outdoor in Charlotte called me and asked if I was planning on going to the OBIEs. She told me that she thought "it would be a very good idea if I came." Hmmm…I thought, *maybe we won more than an OBIE!*

The next day, Gale called back and said that she had spoken with Kevin Gleason, the CEO of Adams Outdoor National, and he'd asked if I would like to be Adams' guest at the OBIEs. Would Claire and I like to fly up to New York on Adams' Gulfstream jet for the ceremony? I immediately accepted, and starting thinking about how I was going to spend my $100,000 (I mean, *our* $100,000, Claire).

On the day of the ceremony we flew up on Adams Outdoor's Gulfstream. Their private jet made first class on US Airways seem like a Trailways bus stuck in the Lincoln Tunnel with no air-conditioning. It was total swankiness. It's the way someone who was about to win 100 Gs would travel. Claire and I checked into the W Times Square, quickly changed into our respective awards outfits, and headed over to the Grand Ballroom at the Trump Hotel for the ceremony.

The emcee announced the OBIE winners, and we were fortunate to win two. One for a campaign for the Charlotte Hornets, and one for a campaign for Carowinds. All OBIE-winning campaigns had a shot at Best of Show. So I figured I had two shots.

Stephen Freitas was welcomed to the stage to announce the winner of the 2002 OBIE Best of Show winner. "In light of the tragic events that took place here in New York on September 11, 2001, the OAAA has decided to donate the $100,000 cash award usually given out to our Best of Show winner to a college scholarship fund for the children of the victims of the egregious attack."

It was a wonderful gesture by the OAAA, and received a thunderous ovation from everyone in attendance.

"Let's have a moment of silence to honor the victims and their families," Stephen said, and we all bowed our heads and thought of the tragedy that had taken place in New York just nine months earlier. Claire and I had lost two friends when the towers fell, and the loss was still very fresh and raw. It was a sobering moment in the midst of an evening of celebration.

"Thank you, everyone," Stephen continued. "And now it is my great pleasure to announce that the 2002 OBIE Best of Show winner is...BooneOakley, for their Charlotte Hornets billboard campaign."

I was honored to win. I was happy...for a second. But then another emotion took over and four words rushed into my head:

Fuck you, bin Laden.

KNOCKOUT

I LIKE GOLF. AND I LIKE WOMEN. But I don't consider either of them a spectator sport. Who wants to sit on the sidelines and watch when playing is so much more fun? A good friend once told me that his two favorite things in life were playing golf and laying women. I'd like to think that I'm better at the latter than the former, but you'd have to ask Claire. She's seen me play golf and she's the only woman I've slept with for the last 25 years. Truthfully, I'm probably a better golfer. And if you've seen me play golf, you have to feel sorry for Claire.

For a small city, Charlotte has more than its share of strip clubs. And in twenty years of living here, I've only been a couple of times. It's not that I have anything against strippers, it's just that I find it kind of boring. It's like watching golf on TV. Yawn.

The only times I've visited a gentleman's club were after I'd been drinking with a bunch of guy friends. It's always somewhere between the fifth or sixth drink that someone yells that five-word rallying cry: "Let's go see some tits!" And it's amazing how guys all react the same way. "Yeah, let's go!" "Get the check now, we're going to a titty bar." And within minutes, you're on your way. That's exactly how it happened one evening, twelve years ago.

A few of my friends and I were out celebrating my buddy Michael's fortieth birthday at The Palm Restaurant. It was a group of five guys and me. They all were from respected professions. Michael was a banker. Ryan was a stockbroker. Matt was a gynecologist. Josh was a plastic surgeon. Nathan was an attorney. These guys had real jobs, and

I was in advertising.

After we had pounded down several vodka tonics, a couple of bottles of very nice red wine, and a cowboy ribeye, we were ready for action. I think it was Ryan who sounded the call: "Time for tits." We paid our tab and piled into the town car that was squiring us around Charlotte that night.

"To the Uptown Cabaret, James," Michael said to the driver. We arrived shortly after eleven, and the place was thumping. We paid the $10 cover charge and crossed into the land of overpriced drinks and overinflated boobs. I think Josh the plastic surgeon particularly liked the experience, not only because he could check out the work of his competitors, but he could pass out business cards to the girls who still had natural breasts. For him, the whole evening was a tax deduction.

Nathan and Ryan headed straight to the private lap dance area. I hung out near the bar and watched the dancers on stage from a safe distance. I drank a Budweiser and was thinking about how much longer it would be before we went home, when I saw a slim brunette working the pole on center stage. I decided that I needed to get a closer look and walked to a seat by the edge of the stage. I ordered another beer, and reasoned that since I was the only one there who hadn't had a lap dance, I'd better get one. Otherwise, I'd have nothing to talk about on the way home.

She was about five foot nine with long, flowing hair that hung to the middle of her back. She was tan with a thin athletic build and she had the most soulful, expressive eyes I'd ever seen. When she finished her time on stage, she walked by, said hello, and introduced herself as Lee. I told her my name was David and that I was pleased to meet her. She asked if I'd like a lap dance and I said that I thought she would never ask.

About that time, "Pour Some Sugar On Me" by Def Leppard filled the room. Lee climbed up in my lap and started moving to the smoky bcat. It's very difficult to have a really hot naked woman gyrating all over you and not be able to touch her. My senses of sight, sound, and smell were filled. But the sense of touch was denied. Even so, I must say that I enjoyed it.

When the song was over, Lee sat in my lap for a minute and asked me if I wanted another dance. I asked her how much, and she said each dance was $25. I told her that I thought that one would do, but before she left, I wanted her to know that I thought she was stunningly beautiful. (I'm sure she had never heard *that* before.) She thanked me and said that she was working hard to keep her little girl in private school. I pretended to be interested, but the last thing that a guy wants to hear about in a strip club is a stripper's kid. I asked what her daughter's name was, and she said Morgan. I told her that was a pretty name and for some reason I asked how old she was. She said she was five.

I said, "I'll bet she'll be a knockout when she grows up, just like her mom."

"You're so sweet," Lee said and gave me a hug. I handed her $25. "I've got to get back up on stage. Thanks."

I gazed in wonderment as Lee sashayed back toward the pole. My hypnotic trance was rudely interrupted by Ryan slapping me on the arm. "Now *she* is really hot, Dave. You really seemed to be enjoying it," he said with a possum-faced grin. I did enjoy it. But I didn't enjoy the thought of him enjoying watching me enjoy it. That is one thing about strip clubs that totally weirds me out. Other people watching guys get into the strippers. The guys always look so strange, totally dressed and the women totally naked. All the guys are acting like if they were naked they would be giving the stripper the ride of her life. Which all of us know isn't true. If the guys were naked, the strippers wouldn't come near us. Strippers hate the guys who come to strip clubs. Well, most of them. I'm sure the girl that Nathan was spending time with didn't hate him. Nathan had been gone for at least 45 minutes when he suddenly appeared. He was extremely agitated.

"Dave, how much did that lap dance set you back?" he asked.

"25 bucks."

"Was it for one song?" he asked.

"Yeah, why?"

"Well, I was upstairs with Tiffany and she gave me a lap dance. The song ended and another one started, and she kept dancing. Then she sat in my lap for a while and then asked me if I wanted her to keep dancing. And I said 'Sure.'"

"She must have been smoking hot," I said.

"She wasn't that hot," Nathan replied. "So she kept going for a couple more songs. After about a half an hour total, she asked again if I wanted her to dance more and I said, 'No thanks, how much do I owe you?' She said $250. I told her that I didn't have $250 and she asked if I had a credit card. I told her that I wasn't putting this charge on my credit card, and she told me to wait there and in a minute she walked back with Dwight, the biggest, scariest, most tatted-up bouncer I have ever seen. Dwight looked at me and said, 'Tiffany says you are refusing to pay.' I didn't want to get my ass kicked, so I handed him my credit card. Look at this," Nathan said as he handed me a credit card slip.

I couldn't help laughing. He was charged $250.

"I hope you at least got something out of it," Ryan said.

"I didn't get anything but a $250 boner."

Josh, who had been listening to Nathan, then delivered the universal pronouncement that signifies it's time to leave a titty bar: "Fuck this place. Let's get out of here." We laughed the whole way home about Nathan and Tiffany. But the real humor had yet to begin.

A few days after our visit to the Uptown Cabaret, Nathan's wife Elise went to the mailbox to get the mail. Waiting for her was their monthly Visa statement. Luckily for Nathan, when you charge something at the Uptown Cabaret, it doesn't say "The Uptown Cabaret" on your bill. There was a charge to Dix Bar and Grill. For $250. I would have paid at least $250 to be a fly on the wall when Elise asked Nathan what that charge was for. He told us that he played it cool and told her that it was a client lunch, and that he had mistakenly put it on their personal card and not his business Amex. He says she bought it. I'm not so sure.

There is an old country song from the 1980s that says, "If you're going to cheat, don't cheat in our hometown." I think it should be updated for the 2000s with a slight lyrical twist: "If you're going to go to a strip club, don't go to a strip club in our hometown." It certainly got Nathan in a bit of hot water. But truthfully, his ten-lap dance experience could have taken place anywhere. But what happened to me after our Uptown Cabaret visit was without a doubt a hometown special.

I had volunteered to be a parent helper in Lucas' art class at Saint Gabriel's Catholic School. I was a little nervous, not really knowing what to expect from twenty-seven five-year-olds. Would it be a classroom of wild hellions slinging finger paint at each other, or would they all be eating glue?

I wish it had been that relaxing.

I was the first parent there and the teacher, Miss Sullivan, was happy to see me. So were the other kids. "Hey, it's Lucas' dad," the kids said almost in unison. "Hello, Lucas' daddy," said a cute little girl. Lucas was very proud that I was there, and took me to his desk and showed me all of his stuff. Miss Sullivan handed me a bag of macaroni, a bag of paper plates and some Elmer's glue. I asked if I was supposed to eat this and the little girl said, "No, sit at this table and make art with it." So I sat down with Lucas and three of his friends. We started creating macaroni art.

I was focused on the creations that were coming together when I heard a woman's voice say, "Oh, there you are, Morgan."

"Hi, Mommy," said the little girl at our table. When I looked up, I thanked God that I was sitting down. If I hadn't been sitting, I would have fainted. Right in front of me, giving her daughter a big hug, was a drop-dead gorgeous brunette.

Suddenly, the memory of our visit to the Uptown Cabaret came rushing back to me. Lee had a daughter. She was in kindergarten. She was working hard to keep her in private school. And her name was Morgan. *Holy shit. Holy shit. Holy shit.*

As soon as they finished hugging, the precocious Morgan said, "Mommy, this is Lucas."

"Oh, hi Lucas," Lee said as she tousled his blond hair.

"Hi," he said back, completely wrapped up in his macaroni.

"And this is Lucas' daddy," Morgan said. "He's nice."

Lee looked at me and I looked at her. I knew exactly who she was, and I was sure that she knew who I was.

"Hi, I'm Lee," she said and extended her hand to me. We shook hands and she said, "Is Morgan being a good girl?"

"Umm…yes, yes, she is," I stuttered. "I'm David, Lucas' dad. Nice to meet you." She looked at me and I at her for a beat longer than normal when you meet someone for the first time.

She smiled and said, "Nice to meet you, too."

Miss Sullivan interrupted and asked Lee if she would help with the finger painting on the other side of the classroom. "C'mon, Mommy, let's go finger paint," Morgan said, and the two of them sashayed across the room.

I spent the next forty-five minutes or whatever was left of art class in a state of shocked disbelief. I must have stared at Lee more in the classroom than I did in the strip club. A thousand thoughts ran through my mind. *Did she remember me? How could she not remember me? She danced naked in my lap a week before. But she had probably given fifty or more lap dances since I got mine. No way she remembers me. I could have been anyone. Relax. There's no way she would remember me. I looked like every other idiot who goes to the Uptown Cabaret.* Well, not exactly. This is Charlotte, and 80 percent of the guys here are clean-cut bankers, lawyers, doctors, and financial planners. I have long blond hair. And there aren't that many guys with long blond hair in Charlotte. *Oh my God, she probably knows Claire. Claire comes to all of these school events. Holy shit balls! One of Claire's friends gave me a lap dance. She's going to tell Claire. She's going to tell Claire.* I was freaking out. *Breathe, David, breathe.*

Suddenly, a calm came over me. First of all, Claire would probably laugh about it. And then I realized that it didn't matter whether Lee remembered me or not. Even if she did, she wasn't going to tell anyone. Why would she? She doesn't want everyone at Saint Gabriel's to know she's a stripper.

Then I heard Miss Templeton say, "It's almost nine thirty. Time to clean up." When the bell rang, I couldn't resist walking over to Lee and saying, "When Morgan grows up, she's going to be a knockout."

She turned, smiled and said, "You know, I've heard that before."

I never saw her again. And I haven't been to a strip club since. Well, not in Charlotte, anyway.

VISA LAS VEGAS

'VE USED THE SAME CREDIT CARD FOR THE PAST FIFTEEN YEARS: THE US AIRWAYS DIVIDEND MILES MASTERCARD. It gives you one mile for every dollar you spend on anything. Over the years, I've racked up quite a few frequent flier miles. Enough to fly to Las Vegas for free every year for March Madness. I love Vegas (some say I'm obsessed), and I go there each year with a group of my best guy friends for the first round of the NCAA basketball tournament. It is my favorite trip of the year, and I would tell you all about it, but, well, you know what they say about what happens in Vegas, right? How could I disregard the advice of such a brilliant campaign?

So anyway, no amount of advertising could ever convince me to try another credit card. It doesn't matter how much I like Tina Fey, I'm not switching to American Express. And no matter how many times Alec Baldwin or his crazy medieval marauder friends ask "What's in your wallet?" my answer will always be the same: "Not a Capital One Rewards card."

So when my cousin Brad Oakley told me that I should think about getting a Total Rewards Visa card from Caesars Palace, I just laughed and said, "I already get frequent flier miles. I fly for free every time we go to Vegas."

"Yeah, I know, Dave," Brad said, "but you can stay for free in Vegas with the Total Rewards Visa card. I just got one and I get double points for groceries and gas."

"I guess that's good," I said, but I wasn't anywhere near being convinced that I should get one.

"Plus," he said, "You get double points for every flight you book."

"Oh, that *is* good," I said, thinking about how much I have to travel sometimes.

"But the best thing about the Total Rewards Visa card is that every month, they feature a retailer on their website and you can get even more points. This month it's Lowe's. For every dollar you spend at Lowe's, you get five points. I just bought a washing machine for $500. That's 2500 points."

I still wasn't convinced, but that evening, I went on the Total Rewards Visa website. They were now featuring Under Armour, and every dollar spent got ten points. Then I saw that 1-800-FLOWERS had a fifteen-points-for-every-dollar-spent deal. Knowing that Valentine's Day was only a month away, I applied for a card on the spot.

CAESARS SHOULD GIVE MY COUSIN BRAD FREE ROOMS FOR LIFE. HIS WORD-OF-MOUTH ADVERTISING NOT ONLY GOT ME TO SIGN UP FOR A TOTAL REWARDS VISA CARD, IT GOT ME TO WRITE THIS STORY, WHICH IS GOING TO BE READ BY MILLIONS, I TELL YOU, MILLIONS! HOOK COUSIN BRAD UP, CAESARS! AND ME TOO, WHILE YOU'RE AT IT!

As advertised, my new card arrived within five business days. The first day I had it, I ordered flowers for Claire. $60 times fifteen points equals 900 points. I was off to the races. (Or should I say, off to the free rooms in Vegas?) I then ordered flowers for my mom, Claire's mom, and my Aunt Hallie. We had a TV shoot coming up for Bojangles', and I put all of the agency's flights on the card. I was racking up the points! I even ordered two sofas for the office and paid for them with the TR card.

I could see it now. This March, we would be staying in the suite they used in the movie *The Hangover* at Caesars Palace. For free.

The following Friday, Claire, Lucas, and I went to Chapel Hill for a three-day weekend. We visited Sydney, who was a sophomore at UNC at the time. I put two tanks of gas, two nights at the Aloft, dinner at Spanky's, and Sydney's spring tuition on the card. Obsessively piling up the points. When we were driving back into Charlotte, I suggested for the first time in my life that we stop at the Harris Teeter before we got home to buy the week's groceries. Claire seriously

Everyone should carry this card. This isn't a paid product placement yet, but it will be after the Total Rewards Visa card gives me a free suite at Caesars Palace every March for the rest of my life. Right, Total Rewards?

thought that I had been abducted by aliens because I hate grocery shopping. But I didn't consider it shopping any more. It was prepping for Vegas.

When we got home, our ten-year-old yellow lab, Yogi, was waiting for us on our back deck. He had his paws up on the fence, wagging his tail, so excited to see us. Our neighbors, the Smiths, had been taking care of Yogi while we were away. Nancy Smith walked over from next door as we drove in. She asked us how old Yogi was. She said that she thought that he had slowed down a lot since she had last dog-sat him. "Maybe he was just missing the Oakleys," she said.

Yogi was wagging his tail furiously and seemed fine to us.

Over the next couple of days, though, we did notice that he was having a little trouble getting up, and wasn't eating quite as voraciously as labs do. So Claire decided to take him to the vet just to make sure everything was OK. The vet seemed a little concerned and did some blood work on him. She told us we would have the results in a couple of days.

Exactly two days later we were told that Yogi had diabetes, and that there was a real possibility that he would be blind within a year. Our vet explained to us that dogs can live a good life with diabetes, but that we would have to give him insulin shots twice a day. Needles are not something that either of us is exactly comfortable with, but we watched Dr. Kim give Yogi his first shot, and she taught us how to do it. We would do anything for that dog. Even stick a needle in him twice a day if it meant that we could spend more time with him.

For the next couple of weeks, we got into the routine of giving Yogi his insulin shots in the morning and in the evening with dinner. But there was a slight problem: he didn't seem to be getting better. The insulin was not bringing Yogi's energy back. He was becoming more lethargic every day. We called the vet, and she asked that we bring him in again for more tests.

This time the results were worse. Yogi had lymphoma. Cancer. It was in his liver and his kidneys and was spreading. It was only a matter of time before he left us. We brought him home and loved on him like always. He was the best dog and friend you could ever ask for. But day by day, he got weaker. By the weekend, he couldn't even stand up. I had to pick up this proud animal and carry him outside and then hold him up so he could do his business. It was so painful to watch his decline.

Everyone says that it's a difficult decision to make the choice to put your pet down. But I believe it was much more difficult for him to be in such pain. It certainly was hard for us to see him that way. Imagining Yogi taking the Rainbow Bridge to doggie heaven was comforting, but it didn't stop the tears from flowing.

We made an appointment for one o'clock on a Friday to put Yogi to sleep. That morning, Lucas called from school and wanted to come home early. His stomach was upset and he was a wreck, as were both Claire and I. When Lucas got home, we asked if he wanted to go to the vet with us. To my surprise, he wanted to come.

I lifted Yogi and put him in the backseat with Lucas and started driving to South Park Animal Hospital. It was the quietest family trip I remember. I looked in my rearview mirror and saw Yogi resting his head on Lucas' lap. I flashed back to ten years earlier, driving back from Goldsboro with our new puppy resting his head on Lucas' lap in the back seat. That's where the then-seven-year-old Lucas named him. "He looks like a Yogi to me." Tears rolled down my face as I thought about how Lucas was holding him when he arrived, and now when he was leaving our lives. Before I knew it, we were at the vet. Dr. Kim and her assistant came outside to help get Yogi inside.

Claire, Lucas, and I each said our good-byes to our loyal friend. I held Yogi's head in my hands as Dr. Kim gave him his final shot. His eyes closed and his head grew heavy. Quickly and painlessly, he fell asleep. He was gone. Yogi was finally at peace.

We drove home in almost complete silence again, except for the occasional sniffle or nose blowing. "We forgot to get his collar," Claire said. "I want to keep his collar. It has his nametag on it." When we got home, I called and they said that they would keep the collar for us.

The next morning I drove back to South Park Animal Hospital to get his collar. "I'm so sorry for your loss. Yogi was a wonderful dog," the receptionist said to me as she handed me his collar.

"Yes, he was," I replied, trying my best not to tear up again. Then I said, "I think I should settle up our bill."

"OK, Mr. Oakley, for the lab work and the euthanasia, the total comes to $387."

Damn, $387, that's a lot of money, I thought. But Yogi was worth every penny. I loved that dog. And he loved me. That's why I knew that Yogi was smiling down from doggie heaven when I whipped out my Total Rewards Visa card to pay for putting him to sleep.

Viva Yogi. Visa Las Vegas.

PART FOUR
CONSTANT CRAVING

CONGRATULATIONS. You are now three-quarters of the way through this book. You have made it farther than anyone so far except for my editor, and she was paid to read the whole thing. (At least I think she read the whole thing.)

Constant craving. k.d. lang sang about it. We all have experienced it. That insatiable desire, that urge, that need that has to be filled. That hunger for something that you just have to have right now. Like a Cajun Filet biscuit. Or a bowl of dirty rice. We learned that firsthand when we developed the "It's Bo Time!" campaign. Constant craving has always been.

From the perspective of the grizzled old ad vet that I now am, the next few stories will explain how I came to understand the power of social media, and how we harnessed it to help land my favorite account ever: Bojangles'. It will also take you behind the scenes on how we developed the "It's Bo Time!" campaign.

THE BEST SIX-CHARACTER TWEET EVER

I SAW THE CONNECTIVE POWER OF SOCIAL MEDIA UP CLOSE AND PERSONAL LAST NIGHT. I was on Twitter and a tweet came up from Rosanne Cash. She had just changed her profile picture to a shot of her onstage playing the guitar. The photo was taken from behind Rosanne on stage with the audience in front of her. Rosanne's tweet referenced her new photo and said, "It's a nice backside, right?" I couldn't resist a silly tweet back, "Your backside rocks. But your front side rocks in the free world."

David Oakley @oakleydavid · 10h
@rosannecash **Your backside rocks. But your front side rocks in the free world.**
     16   11

A minute later Rosanne Cash responded to my tweet. It was the best 6-character tweet ever.

Rosanne Cash @rosannecash · 10h
@oakleydavid **hehhee.**
     5   11

"Hehhee."

I was in shock. Rosanne Cash actually responded to my tweet. How cool was that? I thought it was very cool. So did my friend from Indianapolis, Charlie Hopper.

Charlie Hopper @CharlieHopper · 10h
@oakleydavid **Hey, you made Rosanne laugh.**

🔄 1   ⭐ 1   •••

Charlie tweeted, "Hey, you made Rosanne laugh."

Her response completely made my night. I made Rosanne Cash laugh. Or at least I gave her a chuckle. I couldn't believe it.

It made me think about my dad, Sid. My dad introduced me to her dad's music when I was a kid. And when my kids were small, I introduced Sid to Rosanne's music.

My dad Sid and I went to the 1988 Country Music Awards in Nashville. A friend had given him backstage passes and I flew down from New York to have a father-son weekend with him. I met some of my favorite musicians that weekend: Lyle Lovett, k.d. lang, Loretta Lynn, Dwight Yoakam, and even John Denver.

But by far, the highlight of the weekend was seeing my dad talking with Johnny Cash in a backstage hallway. Then the two of them walked off together. About ten minutes later, my dad showed back up with a giant smile on his face. "Where have you been?" I asked.

"I was just smoking a cigarette with Johnny Cash."

"What?! How did that happen?"

"I introduced myself to him and he noticed my Camels in my front pocket and he asked if he could bum one. I said 'Sure,' and he said, 'C'mon with me,' and he took me out to the fire escape, and we had a smoke."

"What did you talk about?" I asked, amazed.

"He asked how old I was and I told him I was old enough to smoke. He said Johnny laughed and said he figured that. We realized that we were both born in 1932 and had similar backgrounds, growing up poor sharecroppers. I told him that I had come to Nashville for the weekend with my son and he told me he wished he saw more of his kids." My father was beaming. It was a special moment.

A few years back, Rosanne Cash released an album called *Black Cadillac*. Most of the songs on this album are about her relationship with her father and how hard it is coming to terms with the fact that he's not around anymore. Whenever I hear Rosanne Cash sing about her dad, I can't help but think of my father. Her song "God is in the Roses" is one of the most beautiful songs ever written.

Soon after *Black Cadillac* was released, I flew from Charlotte to LA for a shoot. On the flight I listened to the album for the first time. And the second time. And the third time. And the fourth time. And the fifth time. Yes, I listened to it five times in a row. (It's a long flight.) Listening to that album really made me feel really close to my father, who passed away about ten years ago—four months after Johnny Cash.

When I got to my hotel in Los Angeles, I put my bag in my room and then went downstairs to grab a bite to eat. I stopped for a moment in the lobby to look at a magazine when a couple of people walked in to check in. I could tell that they were musicians because they, well, were dressed like musicians and a lot of musicians stay at the Sunset Marquis. I didn't recognize them. Then a third person walked in and I knew instantly who it was. It was Rosanne Cash. I stood about thirty feet away, checking them out. Maybe I was staring. I made eye contact with Rosanne for a moment and she smiled. I'm not sure what she was thinking. Either *That guy is really hot*, or *Who is that weirdo?* Probably the latter. She looked away and I walked over to the restaurant to eat.

Normally I'm very outgoing, so I kind of surprised myself by not introducing myself and telling her the experience that I had just had on the plane. I think I realized that the experience really wasn't between Rosanne and me. The experience was with my dad. Rosanne's music was a conduit that brought us together in a spiritual way. And of course, I think God had a little to do with it. Why else would I be running into her?

For a while, I really regretted not telling her about it. But things happen for a reason. Maybe I wasn't supposed to tell her about it. Maybe she was supposed to read it.

Just like I read her six-character tweet last night.

About a year after that trip to LA, Claire surprised me with two tickets to see Rosanne Cash in Charlotte. Rosanne was playing at Spirit Square, a small venue downtown that used to be a church. It's a wonderfully intimate place to see a show.

We had seats in the third row and the performance was top notch. Rosanne performed with her husband, John Leventhal, one of the most talented guitarists around. They played an all-time favorite of mine, "Long Black Veil," and did an amazing cover of Bobbie Gentry's "Ode to Billie Joe."

This show was especially special to me. Wait a minute. Is especially special redundant? Who cares? The show was especially special to me for a couple of reasons. I love Rosanne's music, and I'd written a blog a few months before about how her album *Black Cadillac* had helped me spiritually in dealing with the passing of my father.

After her encore, Rosanne said that she would come out to the lobby to sign copies of her CDs and her new book, *Composed*.

Claire and I decided to stick around to meet her. We waited in line for about twenty minutes until it was our turn to say hello—the final fifteen minutes of which was spent waiting for the guy in front of us, who asked Rosanne to sign about twenty-five different CDs. Can you say *eBay*?

When it was our turn, I greeted her with a big, almost stalkeresque grin. I was psyched to meet her. "I just want to thank you for coming to play in Charlotte," I said, "It's a wonderful holiday gift for us."

"Thanks, I'm really enjoying it here," Rosanne replied.

"I just want you to know how great it is to finally meet you. I wrote a blog a few months back about listening to *Black Cadillac* on a flight…"

— 224 —

"And then you went to your hotel and saw me," she said, and then turned to her manager. "This is the guy who flew to LA and listened to *Black Cadillac* the whole flight, landed and went to his hotel and there I was in the hotel lobby."

"I remember you telling me about that," her manager replied.

Rosanne then looked back at me and said, "You listened to my music and then you conjured me up. You just conjured me up."

I just stood there grinning I guess, because I couldn't believe she had read my blog and remembered it. And then I said, "It's an awesome album. It made me feel really close with my dad. And thanks for reading my blog."

"Oh, I love your blog. Keep writing."

As we were leaving, I thanked Claire for surprising me with such an awesome present. And then I thought about Rosanne's words. "You just conjured me up."

I haven't heard anyone say those words since my dad Sid died. Sid used to sit in his pottery studio and say, "C'mon, Dave, we need to sell some pots. Conjure us up some customers."

Somehow Rosanne knew.

Rosanne Cash, Claire, and me—notice that Claire is pointing at my Polo logo.

GIVING IT AWAY

AFEW YEARS AGO, I WAS RELAXING ON THE COUCH AT HOME, FLIPPING THROUGH THE CHANNELS, WHEN A STORY ON THE NEWS STOPPED ME. It was something about Lance Armstrong and the Tour de France. I'm not really sure why I stopped on that channel because I can't imagine anything more boring than watching someone ride a bike. Sorry, it's just not a spectator sport. Plus, I was sick and tired of seeing Lance Armstrong and those ubiquitous yellow Livestrong bracelets everywhere. I mean, how could anyone like Lance Armstrong? He dumped Sheryl Crow, for God's sake. How do you dump Sheryl Crow? She's smoking hot *and* she can sing *and* play the guitar. There's nothing in the world hotter than a woman who can play guitar. Maybe she was too hot for him. Maybe Lance wears yellow all the time to signify that he's afraid of her hotness. I don't know. But I do know that at the time, I went out and bought a black *Live Wrong* bracelet just to show my disgust.

Anyway, the story on the news was about a machine called the Nike Chalkbot that was printing messages on the route of the Tour de France. Of course, the messages were in yellow. And the video showed the Tour de France bikers riding over the messages. *What a stupid idea*, I thought. *Those bikers can't read those messages when they're riding over them at 25 or 30 mph. It would be*

FOR THE RECORD, I WAS RIGHT ABOUT LANCE ARMSTRONG.

I THOUGHT HE WAS AN ASS LONG BEFORE THE WORLD FOUND OUT.

like trying to read a billboard with fifty words on it. It's impossible. All the riders could possibly see was a yellow blur under their tires. I rolled my eyes and changed the channel.

About an hour later, I looked out our front window and saw our neighbor Bobby mowing his parents' grass. I remembered that I owed him $20 for dog-sitting the previous weekend, so I decided with nothing on TV, now was as good a time as any to walk over and pay him. It also gave me an excuse to stop in and say hello to his parents, our good friends Sharon and Jeff.

I knocked on their door and Sharon waved me in.

"I brought Bobby's money for watching Yogi last weekend."

"Thanks. Just put it on the table. He'll get it when he finishes the grass. How are you doing, Dave?"

"I should be asking how are *you* doing? You're the one who's been dealing with chemo."

"I'm doing OK. And honestly, I'm starting to like wearing this do-rag on my head. It's kind of stylish," she said with a laugh, "In a Carol Burnett type of way."

"I think you got more of a bad-ass rapper look. More like Eminem or 50 Cent."

"You want some iced tea?" Sharon's iced tea was almost as good as Bojangles'.

"I'd love some."

"I just made a fresh pitcher. It's in the fridge. Help yourself."

I walked into the kitchen and there on the refrigerator was a photo that stopped me in my tracks. It was a picture that was printed from a computer. It was a shot of a road with yellow writing on it that said: "Cancer is no match for my mom. Love Bobby." I stared in stunned silence for a good minute, and then asked, "Where did you get this picture?'"

Sharon answered me back with sheer glee in her voice. "Can you believe what Bobby did for me? He emailed this message to the Livestrong people who are sponsoring the Tour de France, and they painted it on the street in France. This message is on the actual route that the bikers take. It's right outside Chablis."

"Wow," was all I could say. This was incredible. It never occurred to me to make a connection between my friend who had breast cancer and Lance Armstrong.

"Come check this out," she said. She picked up her laptop and I sat down beside her on her sofa and took a sip of sweet tea. She typed in *wearyellow.com.* At the top of the site it said, "Send your message of inspiration to be printed on the Tour de France." And there was a map. Not of France. But of Charlotte. And it had yellow dots all over it. If you clicked on the dots, you could see messages of hope that had been sent from our city. She clicked on one that was sent from Wood-bridge. It was Bobby's message.

"How awesome is that, Dave?"

"Wow," I said again.

At that moment I realized what an idiot I was. The messages weren't meant for the bikers. They were meant for the people who were fighting the disease.

"How did you find out about it?"

"I found out when Bobby gave me the picture. He handed it to me last Tuesday when I walked in the door from my last chemo session." Sharon was beaming.

I had chills. This was real. This was human. This just might be the best viral ad campaign ever and I, supposedly such a cutting-edge ad guy, was absolutely clueless about it.

"How'd Bobby find out about it?"

"He saw it on Facebook or Twitter."

"Unbelievable!" I stood up and gave her a hug.

The door opened and in walked a sweaty Bobby dribbling a basketball.

"Nice Livestrong message," I found myself saying as I gave him a big high-five.

He grinned and said the way only a seventeen-year-old could, "I think Mom liked it."

"She sure did," Sharon said, and smiled.

"Thanks for the tea," I said as I walked out the door. But they had given me much more than tea. They had helped me understand what all the Livestrong fuss was about.

It was so much more than just another Nike marketing scheme. It was real and it was connecting with real people who were battling cancer. Nike was spreading a feeling of hope and unity that together they could win the fight against this horrible disease.

I marveled at how only a few hours before, I had totally dissed the campaign. I thought I knew a thing or two about advertising. I thought I had my finger on the pulse of viral marketing. But I didn't read about this on Adfreak.com or Adcritic.com. I heard about it from a neighbor who's a part-time real estate agent who hasn't left her house in weeks except to go out for chemotherapy. Holy mackerel. This might be the most amazing marketing campaign of all time.

As I walked across the street back to our house, I wondered to myself about Nike. What was it that they were selling? What was the product? If you work on Livestrong, do you get free product?

It occurred to me that Nike was selling *hope*. And what an awesome product it is: Hope that Sharon can beat this disease. Hope that she will be around to see Bobby's high school graduation. Hope that she'll always be here to hug him. Hope is the most wonderful product that anyone could ever sell.

Then it really hit me. Nike isn't *selling* hope. Nike is giving it away. Wow.

Talk about impact. The Livestrong Chalkbot idea punched me right in the face. But what I felt was nothing compared to how Sharon, Jeff, and Bobby were affected. Nike connected with them on an emotional level that few or any other brands ever have. It was human. It was honest. And it was real. It was a Real. Big. Idea.

IF THE COLONEL HAD OUR RECIPE,
HE'D BE A GENERAL

WE WEREN'T EVEN SUPPOSED TO BE IN THE PITCH. The new business consultant that Bojangles' had hired to run the agency search had recommended that they send an RFP (Request for Proposal) to sixteen agencies. They had selected their favorite sixteen. At the last minute, Randy Poindexter, the marketing director at Bojangles', asked the consultant to add one more agency to the RFP list. "I told her that BooneOakley had sent me a poster about a year ago and I've got it hanging in my office. I think they at least deserve a shot." That poster was about as simple as you could get. It had a Bojangles' logo with a headline above it that read, *If the Colonel had our recipe, he'd be a General.*

The poster was one part of a seven-year quest to win that piece of business. I love Bojangles'. Love their biscuits. Love their sweet tea. And I especially love their dirty rice. Seven years earlier, we had a golden opportunity to win the account, but I screwed it up. Royally.

How did I blow it, you ask? Simple. We were invited to pitch the account and we accepted. We were told that there would be a question-and-answer get-together for all the invited agencies at the Bojangles' offices on Wednesday the 10th. I marked it on my calendar in red ink. The problem was I marked the meeting for Wednesday the 17th. On Tuesday the 16th, I called Bojangles' to confirm our meeting. I was informed that we wouldn't be moving to the next round of the pitch process, because we hadn't attended the Q&A meeting. I was devastated. Crushed. I couldn't believe that I was so stupid. I had let the entire agency down. I vowed that if the account ever came up for review again, we would win it.

In 2010, we got our chance. Randy remembered our poster and added agency number seventeen to the RFP list. When I got this RFP, I was eating my first Bojangles' meal in over a month. I had just returned from my annual physical and my cholesterol level was at a nice low level, so I treated myself to a Supremes Combo with a large iced tea. Oh, who am I kidding? I would have been eating at Bojangles' even if my cholesterol was at an all-time high. I love me some Bo.

The RFP was pretty standard. Who are the principals at the agency? What accounts do you currently have? How long have you had them? What is your creative process? We filled out every answer meticulously and delivered it to Bojangles' two days before the deadline. I wasn't taking any chances this time.

A week later, we got a call from Debra Mager, the new business consultant, who told me that we had made the cut to the next round. The field had been narrowed to seven. The next step was for the Bojangles' team to visit each of the agencies for a capabilities presentation. Their goal was to get to know a little about each of their cultures.

This was great. It was our turn to shine. We then did something that we hadn't done in a few years. We actually cleaned the agency. Got rid of all our old comps. Straightened our desks. And even threw the science projects out of the refrigerator. (Maybe we should have left them in there since it was a "chemistry check.")

Since we were playing a home game, we decided to have the meeting on our basketball court. It was their opportunity to see if they liked us. And we sure wanted to them to like us.

Randy Kibler, Randy Poindexter, designer Kelsey Moore, and

Mike Bearss from Bojangles' joined us for the meeting, along with Debra Mager. We gave them a tour of BooneOakley and introduced them to everyone, including Yogi and Nebula, the agency pups.

We showed them some work we had done for Ruby Tuesday and State Farm, then talked a bit about our strategic and media capabilities.

"I noticed that you guys have gained a lot of new Facebook fans in the last few weeks. Especially since you sent out the RFP. I see that fifteen folks from Wray Ward have become fans, twelve from Erwin Penland, and I believe twenty from Mullen. It makes sense. If you're pitching a piece of business, you should be a fan. I'm sure some of our people have become fans in the last few weeks."

"But I can assure you no one has been Bojangles' fans longer than the folks at BooneOakley. And we have proof. Show 'em, John."

John Boone reached under the table and pulled out a North Carolina vanity license plate. It read *BOJANGLE.*

Randy Kibler's jaw almost hit the table. "How did you get that? I tried to get that plate."

"Well," John said, "it belongs to my daughter. Bo-Berry Biscuits are her favorite food, and when she got her first car five years ago, she applied for and got this plate. We've been fans for a long time."

"Clearly you have," Randy said with a wink.

I sat at the table across from Mike Bearss. He was a tall guy in his mid fifties, stood around six foot three, and had the biggest, bushiest gray mustache that I had ever seen. I wasn't sure what he did at Bojangles', but his card said VP of Research and Development.

I've trained myself over the years to be able to read what clients are writing upside down. So I kept looking at Mike's yellow notepad during the meeting. I couldn't decipher a word. Mike had filled every inch of his yellow pad with doodles and drawings. This was no typical client.

I told him after the meeting that I was trying to read his notes. He told me he does the same thing. I told him that his notes were like a work of art and I couldn't read a word. Then I said, "Since I couldn't read your notes, just tell me what you thought of us." He laughed and said we did a good job and he looked forward to seeing us again soon.

A few days after their visit to BooneOakley, I got another call from Debra Mager. We had made it to the third round. Bojangles' had selected four finalists to present ideas to them in two weeks. First, we had made the Sweet Sixteen on a play-in game. And now we had made the Final Four. We congratulated ourselves for about two minutes, and then briefed the teams on the assignment. But our goal wasn't making the Final Four. It was winning the whole thing.

We worked feverishly for the next fourteen days, creating ideas that we thought would be right for Bojangles', but more importantly would help us win the account. But we knew that the other three agencies would be doing the same thing. You can't win an account on creative alone.

We had to do something different. Something that would set us apart from the competition.

We decided that instead of working on their business, we needed to work *in* their business. Literally. So we called the Bojangles' office and told them that we wanted to work in one of their restaurants. We wanted to learn how to make the biscuits and cook the dirty rice and Cajun Filets. We figured that that experience would influence our work and make it more genuine and authentic. John volunteered. A couple days later, he was working a six a.m. to two p.m. shift at the Bojangles' on North Tryon Street. I visited John at lunch and he told me that it was the hardest that he had ever worked in his life. Which wasn't surprising to me. Not only did I know that the work itself would be hard, I also knew that art directors aren't normally the hardy type. What we did learn was that Bojangles' biscuits are truly made from scratch. They take no shortcuts, and this was learning that directly went into our work. I shot a few photos of John in his flour-covered apron and headed back to the office to meet Craig Jelniker, our agency producer.

That evening, Craig and I hopped on a plane and flew to Alabama. Bojangles' was moving into the Birmingham area and was opening a restaurant in Tuscaloosa. The grand opening was the next morning and we had a plan. We were going to be their first customers. So at five a.m., we showed up with iPhone in hand, filming our arrival. The manager saw us walk in and turned and said to the other workers, "Hey guys, it's our first customer, look sharp." She then turned to us and said, "Welcome to Bojangles'. Good morning. Can I take your order?"

"Are we your first customers?"

"Yes, you sure are, sir."

"Well we've been waiting for a long time for you to open this restaurant. We'll have two Cajun Filet combos and two coffees, please." Craig and I sat down and enjoyed our breakfast, then went over and introduced ourselves to the manager. Her name was Wanda Hart. We told her we were with an ad agency that was trying to win the Bojangles' account and wondered if we could ask her some questions. She was delighted to talk with us. We spent the day interviewing her, and other Bojangles' employees and customers.

At the end of the day, Wanda came over and sat at the booth with Craig and me. "I don't know if I should tell you this, but I called the Support Center in Charlotte (Bojangles' corporate office is called the Support Center) and asked them about y'all."

"You don't believe that we're from an ad agency?" I joked. She laughed and said that she just wanted to make sure we were legit.

"But this is what I wanted to tell you. I asked Randy Poindexter if the other agencies were going to come here to interview me. He said no, we were the only one. Then he told me that someone from your agency worked at a restaurant yesterday. And he said you were the only agency that has done that. It's making a big impression back in Charlotte. If you asked me, it gives you a major leg up on the others."

I liked that they were talking about us at the Support Center. That was a good sign. Now all we had to do was come up with a couple of great campaigns to show them.

Easier said than done. Two days before the pitch we had two campaigns. They were good campaigns. Well, maybe one of them could be good, but it wasn't finished. The other one involved a fox that kept trying to get into Bojangles' like a fox always tries to get in the chicken coop to get the chickens. Good thing that we had made an impression in Tuscaloosa, because at this point our creative work wasn't going to win the business.

The campaign that wasn't done had potential. It was all based on the premise that people crave the flavor of Bojangles' chicken. We had spent a lot of time on Bojangles' social media platforms, especially Facebook, and we were struck by what we saw. Bojangles' restaurants were only in the southeast, but Bojangles' had fans all across the country. These people had ties to the South, but had moved away and could no longer get a Cajun Filet Biscuit. They professed their love for Bojangles' daily and begged them to build restaurants in such places as Billings, Montana, Cedar Rapids, Iowa, and even Alaska. We saw the phrase "Love Me Some Bo" in what seemed like every other post. So we decided to build the campaign around the fans, and made *Love Me Some Bo* our tagline.

Even so, the campaign just didn't seem to be coming together. Something was missing. It needed a spark. Some glue to hold it together. It was forty-eight hours until the presentation.

I went back to my office and did what most creative directors do in a time crunch: I got on Facebook. After liking a few photos that my friends had posted, I went to the Bojangles' page. I scrolled down a little farther and noticed something that I hadn't seen before. It was a video that a fan had posted. I played it and couldn't believe what I was seeing. Then I played it again. It was two guys in their mid-twenties who were singing a song about Bojangles'. It was super lo-fi, shot in one of their bedrooms. One of them was playing a guitar and one was playing a xylophone. But the tune was well-written and very catchy. It was posted by a guy named Sawyer Frye. I went to his Facebook page and saw that he was from Carthage, North Carolina, a small town about ninety minutes east of Charlotte.

I showed the video to John, Craig, Phil Smith, and Demian Brink. They agreed that it was cool and that maybe we should include it in our presentation. I told them I thought we should get them to perform it live at the pitch.

"Good luck with that. It's Tuesday. The pitch is Thursday morning."

Yeah, but as Michael Jordan once said, "Every shot you don't take is a guaranteed miss."

This might have been a shot from the last seat in the last row of the upper deck, but I drafted a Facebook message to Sawyer. I told him that we liked his video and would like to talk with him about using it in a presentation to Bojangles'. I asked him to get back in touch with us as soon as possible.

As soon as I pressed send, the paranoia set in. This was too simple. Too good. This guy probably was hired by one of the other agencies to write and post a song. How embarrassing would that be? Another agency telling Bojangles' in the pitch that they had written a song and it was so good that BooneOakley was trying to get it. I waited and waited to hear back. Nothing. A full twelve hours passed. I was moving to Plan B. I had shot an air ball from the upper deck.

Then it happened. The message icon on my Facebook page illuminated. Sawyer had responded. He said he was flattered that we liked his song. I wrote him back immediately that I would love for him to come to Charlotte and perform it for Bojangles' the next morning at nine o'clock. "I'll put you up in a hotel and pay you," I wrote, "if you can be here tonight." I immediately pressed send. I looked at the message that I had just sent and thought, *That sounds so creepy, I'll be amazed if he responds again.* But he did. He asked if he could bring his brother-in-law, Phillip, who performed with him in the video (probably to be his bodyguard). I said of course, and asked him to send his phone number. He did.

When I finally got Sawyer on the phone, I kept apologizing for how sketchy the Facebook message must have sounded. I promised him that we were a legit agency (although sometimes even I questioned that), and that we would pay him $500 if he showed up and performed the following morning.

"For $500, we'll be there," he said. He asked if he should come by the agency tonight just so he would know exactly where to meet us in the morning. At seven o'clock that evening, Sawyer and Phillip showed up. We were in full frenzy mode, putting finishing touches on our presentation. I led them into the BooneOakley conference room, which we had turned into a Bojangles' pitch war room and introduced them to our team. I think it was Claire who asked, "Why don't you guys do a rehearsal? Let's hear the song." The boys took out their guitar and xylophone and began.

By the time they had reached the chorus, everyone in the room was grinning. Our pitch theater had arrived. And it wasn't just theater, it was live music.

Before I knew it, we were in a giant conference room somewhere in Bank of America Stadium, and I was standing in front of eight Bojangles' executives about to present.

I started by saying that this was the most important presentation in the ten-year history of BooneOakley. I then reached into my pocket and pulled out my phone. I read them a text that my daughter Sydney had just sent me. "'Good luck Dad. I know you'll do great.' Sydney knows how hard we've worked on this. Even with that kind of encouragement, I'm still really nervous standing here in front of you," I said. "This presentation means so much for the agency. It means so much for me. It's a chance to atone for screwing up seven years ago, the last time Bojangles' was up for review. So yes, I'm a little nervous."

Telling the audience how nervous I am is something that I always seem to do when I start presenting. It's kind of my default thing to say when I'm trying to get my thoughts together. It also makes me feel better and I think it helps me connect emotionally. I mean, who hasn't been nervous for a presentation? Admitting it humanizes you. I really believe if an audience thinks I'm a little nervous, they have more empathy for what I have to say and maybe, just maybe, I won't come off as a typical ad douche.

But this time, I really was nervous.

"You guys have done some outstanding work in the last seven years," I continued. "I loved your tagline when it came out. It was catchy, but it had one problem: I could never remember it. When I try to say it I always say it wrong." I stopped and said it out loud twice. "'Gotta Wanna Needa Gotta Bojangles.' Wait. 'Gotta Wanna Needa Getta Bojangles.'" Both times I said it wrong. "See? I'm in front of the top execs from Bojangles' and I can't even get the line right. And I'm in advertising. And I've been practicing. For that reason, we recommend that you move away from that line. It's served you well for the last seven years. But it's grown tired. And I still can't say it. So it's time to drop it and go with something new."

I put up a slide with four words on it: *Love Me Some Bo.* "Love Me Some Bo," I said, and then repeated it. "It's a line straight from your customers. It's real. It's authentic. And it's got your name in it. We heard people say it in Alabama. In Raleigh. There's a true love affair between your food and your customers. People love Bojangles'. But the place people are really saying it, or writing it, is on Facebook. There are literally hundreds of posts of people professing their love of the brand with the phrase 'Love me some Bo.'

"Not only are they writing and talking about you on Facebook, they're singing about you." I clicked to a slide of Sawyer and Phillip with their guitar. "I'm sure you guys have seen these guys." I looked at Randy Poindexter and said, "You've seen 'em, right, Randy?" Randy smiled and said no. I looked at Randy Kibler, the CEO, and asked, "Randy, you've seen Sawyer, haven't you?" He smiled and said that he hadn't. "People are talking about you. People are writing about you. And people are singing about you. Right on your Facebook page. On your very own page. We need to put them to work. Let them tell the story of Bojangles' to the world."

Sawyer Frye and Phillip Searcy, who accepted my Facebook invitation and joined us for the Bojangles' pitch.

I pointed the clicker at the screen and tried to get the screen shot of Sawyer and Phillip to play. Nothing happened. "I want you guys to hear the song that's on your Facebook page." I clicked again. "Darn it. This always happens when I'm presenting." I started to get a little agitated. I looked over at Debra Mager, and said, "Is there an IT person here? This is ridiculous."

She stood up and said, "I can check with the receptionist…"

I interrupted her and said, "No I'll do it myself." I dropped the clicker on the table in front of Mike Bearss for effect, and it bounced twice before landing on his yellow legal pad. I stormed out of the conference room and slammed the door behind me.

I counted to ten and walked back in. "Did you find the IT person?"

Debra asked.

"No I didn't. But I found something better in the lobby. Sawyer and Phillip. Come on in, boys." I led them to the middle of the room, and they sat down on a couple of stools that Phil brought over. They began playing their song live.

> When life is hard and nothing goes your way
> Reach inside your heart and hear the words I say
> You need something to soothe your soul
> Put some dirty rice in your bowl
>
> It's morning time and I need some chicken quick
> Need some seasoned fries and some sweet tea I can sip
> Hurry up I need it now
> Got to get that sweet Bojangles' fix
>
> I remember my first bite of Bo-Berry
> A feeling that was strange, oh how it scared me
> It was a heavenly spasm
> My very first Bo-Gasm
>
> If you're looking for a place that you would like to eat
> Look no further my brother 'cause in the Southern skies you'll see
> A place that will
> Set your taste buds free
>
> Love me some,
> Love me some
> Love me some
> Love me some Bojangles

When they finished, everyone in the room stood and gave Sawyer and Phillip a rousing standing ovation. We thanked them for coming in and led them back out of the conference room. Randy Kibler stood up and looked at me and said, "Now I'm going to leave the room." We all looked around at each other for a moment. I started going over how we would approach their point-of-purchase displays.

A couple of minutes later, Randy walked back in and said, "Sorry about that. I just wanted to make sure those guys knew how much I appreciated them being Bojangles' fans. I gave them my business card and told them I would send both of them $100 Bojangles' gift cards and to stay in touch."

I knew at that moment that we had won the pitch.

We left the meeting exhausted and satisfied. We knew that we had given it our all. Left it all on the field at Bank of America Stadium. Or at least on the conference room carpet.

A week later we got the call that we'd won the Bojangles' account.

We played our game. And Sawyer played the guitar.

Live music always beats PowerPoint.

HIT THE BISCUIT

SOMETIMES THE STARS JUST LINE UP.
Against all odds. Against all obstacles. Against all logic. I'm not sure why this is, but sometimes things work out better than you can ever imagine. It doesn't happen often, but when it does, you damn well better take a minute to appreciate it.

There's no rhyme or reason behind this thing called luck. But I've always heard that luck is what happens when preparation meets opportunity. I can tell you one thing: we weren't prepared for the streak of luck that we encountered on a recent Bojangles' project.

It's common knowledge that the Bojangles' Master Biscuit Maker is the absolute best in the business at making biscuits. But we wondered how the Master Biscuit Maker would fare against masters in other fields. So we developed a campaign that pitted the Master Biscuit Maker against a Master Sergeant, a Master Sensei, a Bass Master, and a Masters Champion.

Laura Wallace, the account supervisor on Bojangles', and I presented the idea to Randy Poindexter, Mike Bearss, and Doug Poppen, the marketing team from Bojangles'. They loved the idea of having a Masters Champion challenge the Master Biscuit Maker in a biscuit-making contest.

"What Masters Champion would you recommend?" Randy asked.

"Bubba Watson," I replied.

"It's the logical choice. Bubba grew up in northern Florida, he went to college at University of Georgia," Laura reasoned. "And his name is Bubba. How perfect is that for a southern chicken and biscuits restaurant?"

"Bubba would be awesome," Randy agreed.

"Do you really think we could get him?" Mike asked.

"We can try," Laura replied, and looked at me with a classic Laura Wallace look: *Maybe we should have thought about whether or not we could really get him before we presented the idea.*

"It's kind of a long shot. But as Laura said, it's worth trying. The worst thing that can happen is that he says no. And what have we lost? Nothing. Let's go for it and if he won't do it, or his price is too high, we'll kill the spot and do a different concept. This idea really doesn't work with anyone else."

That afternoon, we reached out to Bubba's agent and sent her the script. The answer came a couple of days later in an email from another source. Bubba had numerous multimillion-dollar endorsement contracts and wouldn't be interested in appearing in a one-time commercial for a fast food chain.

This was disappointing, but we sent the storyboard to his agent anyway. Laura then sent an email to Randy at Bojangles' that basically said, it's not officially dead, but we think it's dead. She scheduled a presentation a few days later to show replacement ideas to them. We started thinking of alternative Masters to challenge the Master Biscuit Maker. We came up with Master Swordsman, Master Magician, and even Master Baiter. None of them were anywhere as good as the Masters Champion idea.

The day before we were scheduled to show the new work, we got a surprising email from Bubba's agent. Bubba had seen the storyboard and was interested. His agent asked that we set up a call to discuss.

That afternoon, Laura George, our agency producer, Laura Wallace, Anna Lindsey, an assistant account executive, and I got on a conference call with Bubba's agent, Amanda Shaw, in Phoenix. She explained that Bubba would do it for the money we had offered, but on one condition: he wanted to hit a biscuit with his golf club. She explained that Bubba was kind of quirky that way, and thought it would be funny to smash a biscuit. *That's crazy*, I thought. *The client will never buy that. That's desecrating the product we are trying to sell.* I explained to Amanda that we really wanted Bubba to hit the dough, while he was trying to make biscuits. She said that Bubba told her he would do it only if he could hit a biscuit. "Well," I said to her, "I'm not sure it totally makes sense."

"I want to hit a bissssssssss-cuitttttttttttt," a male voice came through the conference room phone. We all looked up from staring at the black box in the middle of the table and looked at each other like *what the heck was that?* Amanda started giggling. "I want to hit a bissssssssss-cuitttttttttttt," the male voice rhythmically said again. "Ahhh…Bubba just walked in," Amanda cackled.

"Hi everybody. Who's on the call? The Bojangles' Biscuit Boys?"

We were all taken off guard. It never occurred to us that Bubba would be on the call.

I now know it's possible to be starstruck on the phone.

"Is this really Bubba?" I skeptically asked.

"Of course it's me. Who else would it be?"

"I don't know…umm…" I said, flustered.

"Well, why are you in Phoenix?" Laura George quickly asked.

"I'm playing in the Phoenix Open here starting tomorrow."

"So you think you might want to do our commercial?"

"I like this commercial, but I want to hit a biscuit in it. Just to watch it explode. Do you know how cool that will be if the biscuit explodes right into the camera? It'll look really cool. I'll do it if I can hit a biscuit."

Scott Corbett, the New York director we had hired to shoot the campaign, got on the call and explained the spot. "Bubba, you'll be on what looks like a kitchen competition show set and you'll be trying to make biscuits better than a Bojangles' Master Biscuit Maker. You'll use your golf club as your tool to make the biscuits. You'll make golf ball–size dough balls and hit them with your golf club into the oven. Even though you try really hard, you lose to the biscuit maker because she is the best at making biscuits."

"Great," Bubba replied, "Then I'll hit the biscuit. After I lose."

"Yeah, but wouldn't you rather just eat the biscuit?"

"No, I want to hit it. Maybe I'll eat a different one."

I had gathered myself a bit by then and said, "We'll let you hit a biscuit if you will hit the dough balls, too."

"OK," he said, "I'll hit both. Deal."

We said good-bye and hung up. I looked around the conference room at Laura, Laura, and Anna. *That was so cool. And random. We were just talking with Bubba Watson! And he agreed to do the spot.*

Now we had to convince Mike and Randy to spend their money to let Bubba destroy their product. What had we just agreed to?

We went over to Bojangles' the next morning, fully expecting to have to do a pretty big sales job to convince them. Laura, who normally is brimming with confidence, confessed to me later that she was completely filled with dread about asking Randy and Mike if they would ever fathom letting Bubba, *gasp*, hit a biscuit. But she sure didn't show it. Even when Bojangles' new CEO Clifton Rutledge joined the meeting.

Laura started the meeting with our rationale. "We believe that Bubba Watson is the perfect spokesperson for the Bojangles' brand," she said. "His Q-Score among our core audience is very high and he's got a great

A Q-SCORE IS A MEASUREMENT ON A SCALE OF 0 TO 100 OF THE FAMILIARITY AND APPEAL OF A BRAND, COMPANY, OR CELEBRITY. THE HIGHER THE Q-SCORE, THE MORE HIGHLY REGARDED THE PERSON IS AMONG THE GROUP THAT IS FAMILIAR WITH THEM. FOR INSTANCE, RONALD REAGAN'S Q-SCORE AMONG GRANVILLE COUNTY REPUBLICANS WOULD PROBABLY BE 100. MINE WOULD BE 0.

reputation among his peers. He's highly respected as a good ol' boy who's a good ol' guy."

This was taken right before I tried to steal Bubba's Swatch—I mean, watch.

"So is he going to do the spot or not?" Randy interrupted.

"We're getting to that, Randy," Laura said with a twinkle-eyed smile. "OK, the bottom line is that Bubba has agreed to do the spot. On one condition." Laura paused for effect, I think. "Bubba wants to hit a biscuit."

"He wants to hit a biscuit?" Randy asked, as he burst out laughing.

"That's the condition?" Mike chuckled.

"I don't have a problem with Bubba hitting a biscuit," Randy said, "Do you, Mike?"

"Not at all. I think it'll be funny as hell."

"Let's do it!" Clifton said.

Laura and I looked at each other with a look that can only be described as, *We didn't see that coming.*

I've never had or heard of a client who thought that destroying their product in a TV commercial would be funny. But I've never worked with a client like Bojangles'.

Three weeks later, we were in a studio in Orlando waiting for our Masters Champion, Bubba Watson, to arrive on the set. You never know what to expect from a celebrity. Would he be a green-M&M's-type guy who stayed in his trailer and only came out when he was on camera? Or would he be a regular person? When he drove up, it was clear the answer was neither. We knew that Bubba owned the original "General Lee" Dodge Charger from the TV show *The Dukes of Hazzard*. But we didn't know that he drove a custom-made, bullet-proof, camouflage Ford F-450 with his biggest sponsor's name, Oakley, across the grill. (I personally took that as a very good sign.)

Bubba came inside the studio and we introduced him to everyone on our team. He was very polite, gracious, and friendly. Scott Corbett brought him over to the set of the cooking show that we had created. Scott explained to Bubba how we were going to shoot him hitting the biscuit.

"I actually already did a couple of test shots of me hitting the biscuit, Bubba," Scott said. "I swung and connected with the biscuit and it just disintegrated. It went everywhere."

Bubba just listened, looking Scott over and nodding his head in agreement.

"I swung pretty hard, but I'd have to think that you swing a golf club a little harder than me. Maybe even twice as hard," Scott said in a complimentary way.

Bubba looked at Scott up and down and said, "I'd say probably that I swing the club at least three to four times as hard as you."

"Why do you say that?"

"Well, you don't really look like much of an athlete to me," Bubba said to Scott with a straight face. There was an awkward moment of silence, and then Bubba busted out laughing. He was totally messing with Scott.

"You're screwing with me, aren't you?" Scott asked.

"Maybe," Bubba replied with a grin. Then they both laughed.

A few minutes later, we were looking at Bubba's final wardrobe, and Laura Wallace, whose attention to detail is unrivaled, asked Randy if Bubba wore a watch while he was playing. Her thought was that if Bubba didn't wear it when he was playing, he shouldn't wear it when he's baking. Randy asked me. I told them that I had no idea, so I mentioned it to Scott. Scott and I walked back onto the set to ask Bubba.

"You don't wear that watch when you play, do you Bubba?" Scott asked.

"Yeah, I do. It's a Richard Mille. They're one of my sponsors."

"Oh, Dave thought it was a Swatch," Scott said.

"A Swatch? Dude, this is a $600,000 watch."

"Now I know you're screwing with me," Scott said with a laugh.

"No seriously, it's a custom-made watch. I never take it off."

I walked back over to where Laura and Randy were sitting. They didn't believe it either, so Laura googled "Bubba Watson Watch" and within seconds had confirmed that the watch was sold for $600,000. He was wearing a watch that's worth more than my house. Clearly, he wasn't doing this commercial for the money. I guess he really liked the idea for the spot. Or maybe he was just bored and wanted to hit a biscuit.

The shoot went along according to schedule. We got all the shots of the Master Biscuit Maker meticulously preparing the biscuits and Bubba unsuccessfully trying to make biscuits with his signature pink driver. We even had Bubba stand on a four-foot-high butcher block and hit the dough balls into the oven. Finally, every shot was in the can, except for one: the money shot.

It was time for Bubba to hit a biscuit. We placed a perfectly prepared biscuit on the concrete floor in front of the set. Bubba's action was to grab his pink driver, walk up to the biscuit, set up, and take a full swing and knock the biscuit to smithereens. He did just that. Six times in a row. Each time the biscuit sat flat on the concrete and each time he destroyed it, sending biscuit shrapnel flying across the studio. Each time he busted the biscuit, the crew exploded in laughter. I laughed the first time, but each subsequent time, I just stared in disbelief. There's a reason this guy is wearing a $600,000 watch. He's good. *Really good.* If I had tried to hit the biscuit six times, the only thing I would have broken was the driver when it hit the concrete on my downswing. Or I would have whiffed.

Bubba then shook hands with everyone, signed autographs, and left the set. I couldn't believe that we had just shot a spot with a Masters Champion. I thought, *it doesn't get any better than this.* But it did.

We flew back to Charlotte and edited the spot over the next few weeks. The final spot was completed and approved by Bojangles' on Tuesday, April 8. We shipped it to TV stations that evening, and it began airing on the first day of the 2014 Masters and ran throughout the weekend.

The fun was just beginning. My friend Ted Williams from the *Charlotte Observer* asked me if I had ever participated in a Masters Calcutta. I told him that I had never heard of a Masters Calcutta. He figured that since I enjoy visiting Las Vegas so much, I would enjoy wagering on the Masters. He said that a group of his friends was going to meet at Angry Ale's the Wednesday night

A "CALCUTTA" DESCRIBES A TYPE OF AUCTION-POOL WAGERING THAT CAN BE APPLIED TO GOLF AND OTHER SPORTING EVENTS. DON'T FEEL BAD. I DIDN'T KNOW WHAT IT WAS EITHER.

before the Masters started, and bid on players in the tournament.

Ted explained that we would start with the fiftieth ranked golfer and bid until we got to the number-one ranked golfer in the world. He said that it would be low stakes. As a general rule, I advise that when someone asks you to come gamble and they say it's low stakes, stay away. It's usually high stakes. But this was Ted, who used to work for me at BooneOakley, and I knew what I paid him then and I didn't think he was making enough for it to be a high stakes event. So I decided to attend.

Ted opened the bidding on the fiftieth ranked player in the world, Francesco Molinari, at $3. Subsequent bids would be in increments of $3. Francesco sold for $3. So did the next five players. Even though the stakes were pretty low, I stayed on the sidelines as the other twenty-two guys bid on the players. By the time we got to the twenty-fifth ranked player, they were going for about $24 to $30 each. Not too expensive. But all the great players were still on the board. Including Bubba Watson. Bubba was ranked #11. Jason Dufner, #14, went for $66. Steve Stricker, #13, went for $57. #12 Jordan Spieth went for $60. Ted announced that we would take a break before we got into the Top Ten, so we had one more golfer before our break: Bubba Watson. I was determined to win Bubba, because we'd had such a great experience with him on the shoot and the spot had come out fantastic. Why not put a little money on him? The bidding began at $3 and Bubba was quickly bid up to $66. I stayed out of the bidding until the very last minute, because I didn't want the others to know that I was interested in him.

Ted shouted, "Jim Doyle has Bubba at $69, going once…going twice…"

"$72," I raised my hand and shouted.

Doyle slapped the table and said "$75."

I yelled, "$78."

It had become a one-on-one bidding war for Bubba.

A minute later I bid $96. Ted shouted, "$96 to Oakley. Going once …going twice…are you in, Jim?" Jim gave the classic blackjack wave hand signal and said, "I'm out."

"Bubba Watson, sold to David Oakley for $96."

I just had a good feeling about Bubba. I hadn't planned on paying $96 for that good feeling, but what the hell? I would have been cheering for Bubba anyway. Why not cheer with a little skin in the game? I promised myself that if Bubba won, I would contribute the winnings to BooneOakley's 401(keg) Plan, and we'd use it to buy a kegerator for the agency.

THE BOONEOAKLEY 401(KEG) PLAN KEEPS BEER SUPPLIED TO EMPLOYEES OF BOONEOAKLEY. EMPLOYEES ARE ASKED TO CONTRIBUTE $10 PER MONTH TO THE PLAN. BOONEOAKLEY MATCHES EMPLOYEE CONTRIBUTIONS 100 PERCENT. IF YOU PARTICIPATE IN THIS PLAN, YOU ARE ELIGIBLE TO DRINK COLD BEER EVERY AFTERNOON STARTING AT 4:01 P.M.

THIS PROGRAM IS COPYRIGHTED INTELLECTUAL PROPERTY OF BOONEOAKLEY, AND IF YOU EVEN THINK OF USING THIS IDEA WITHOUT EXPRESS WRITTEN CONSENT OF BOONEOAKLEY, WE WILL SUE THE LIVING SHIT OUT OF YOU.

When we returned from our break, the bidding on the Top Ten golfers commenced. No one in the Top Ten went for less than $125. The Top Five all went for over $180, and Adam Scott, the number-one ranked player, went for $225. The total pot was $3200. First place would get 50 percent of the pot. *Go, Bubba, go!*

The next four days were nothing short of magical. Bubba took the Masters lead on Thursday and never looked back. He led wire-to-wire and pulled away late on Sunday afternoon to claim his second Masters title in three years.

Laura Wallace (who is one of the biggest sports fans I know) once told me that she didn't attend golf tournaments because she didn't support sports where the spectators are shushed. Let me tell you, there was no one on the Bojangles' team that was abiding by the Quiet Please signs that the officials held up during the 2014 Masters. We were screaming our lungs out at every shot that Bubba made. When he sank the last putt on eighteen to clinch the tournament, and his three-year-old son walked out to hug his dad, I knew that this was as good as it gets. And that we never would have been able to sign Bubba if he had already won two Masters.

For once, we looked kinda like geniuses. But we weren't. And we aren't. We just happened to be very lucky. And sometimes it's better to be lucky than good. Or maybe you make your own luck. But no, Bubba made our luck this time.

Quite simply, the stars just lined up. It was perfect.

Well, almost.

On Monday morning after the Masters, we had to fix a major mistake that we had made on the title card of the spot. It said *Bubba Watson: 2012 Masters Champion.* We changed it to *Bubba Watson: 2012 & 2014 Masters Champion.*

Bubba hit the biscuit and then he ate one—then he won the Masters again.

IT'S BO TIME!

O F ALL THE CAMPAIGNS THAT WE HAVE DONE AT BOONEOAKLEY OVER THE YEARS, I'M PROBABLY MOST PROUD OF "IT'S BO TIME!" FOR BOJANGLES'. It's about as close to a perfect tagline as you can get. It's a rallying cry. It's a call to action. Heck, it's even got the client's name in it. It's short. It's easy to remember. And in the past four years, it's become part of the vernacular in this part of the country. I daresay it's become almost as iconic as the Bojangles' brand itself.

A lot of people assume that "It's Bo Time!" won the Bojangles' business for us. Well, that's not the way it happened. We didn't come up with the line until after we had won the account. A few weeks after we won the business, we had a meeting at Bojangles' with their marketing team.

Randy Kibler started the meeting by saying, "We really like that 'Love Me Some Bo' tagline that you guys presented to us in the pitch. But I'm not sure we really *love* it. It does a great job of summing up how people feel about Bojangles' food. We like it, don't get us wrong, but it just seems a little soft."

Randy Poindexter built off of what Kibler said. "'Love Me Some Bo' doesn't really create that sense of urgency that you guys talked about in your strategy about how people crave our food. I think you guys should go back to the agency and come up with something that is more of a call to action. Something that is more about that moment of being hungry and deciding to go to Bojangles', instead of to Chick-fil-A."

Then Randy Kibler interjected, "I'm not saying that we're not going to go with 'Love me Some Bo,' I'm just saying that I think we should try to beat it."

When the CEO of a company asks you to beat a line, it usually means that tagline is dead. *And just like that, the honeymoon is over,* I thought.

I really loved the "Love Me Some Bo" line. It was real. It had come from what their customers were saying on Facebook. But I was willing to give it a shot. So we headed back to the agency with a job to do.

Over the next couple of weeks, the teams at BooneOakley came up with a couple hundred new taglines for Bojangles'. We narrowed it to fifty, and printed each of them on a sheet of paper and taped them up on the conference room wall. We kept eliminating lines until we were left with four: "Get Some," "Love Me Some Bo," "I'm Cravin' Cajun," and "It's Bo Time!"

I had my doubts about "It's Bo Time!" It reminded me of a line that we had used in the past for the Charlotte Hornets: "It's Bee-Ball Time." It also reminded me of "It's Miller Time." Not only that, I wasn't sure what it really meant. Three simple words. It seemed kind of boring. That is, until Keith Greenstein and Matt Klug brought it to life.

Keith and Matt were a senior writer / art director team at Boone-Oakley. They came into the conference room and said to me, "Here's how we think we can make 'It's Bo Time!' work. It's all in the execution. Imagine that moment when you crave Bojangles' food. At that very instant, it's the most important thing in your life. You've got to get a Cajun Filet immediately. So we think we can do a series of commercials where people drop whatever they are doing and run to Bojangles' to eat. At that moment, nothing is as important as satisfying that craving for delicious Bojangles' food."

"So give me an example," I said.

"There could be thousands of scenarios," Keith responded with kid-like enthusiasm. "OK, imagine a guy down on one knee about to propose to his future wife and his stomach growls, and instead of 'Will you marry me?' he says, 'It's Bo Time!' and leaves her sitting there and runs to Bojangles."

"OK, that's pretty funny," I said to them.

"Or it could be a woman is doing a eulogy at a funeral and her stomach growls she runs out of the funeral because 'It's Bo Time!' for her."

"Or it could be a creative director who runs out of a presentation because he's craving a bowl of dirty rice." I said, totally understanding the legs (no pun intended) that this campaign could have.

"Sure," Matt said. "I think we could come up with a lot more situations."

A few days later, the marketing team from Bojangles' came over to BooneOakley so we could show them our new tagline directions. Before they arrived, we decided to have the meeting on the basketball court for a simple reason. Beside the court was a large window that looked out onto the sidewalk and street outside. We were going to use that view to demonstrate how "It's Bo Time!" worked.

I started the presentation and welcomed Randy K., Randy P., Mike, and Kelsey back to BooneOakley. I told them that we had some great work to share with them. "You guys challenged us to beat 'Love Me Some Bo,' and I'm hoping by the end of this meeting you'll think that we have." I then invited Keith and Matt to come up and present the new tagline.

Keith started talking about what a big moment this was for us as an agency. To be tasked with coming up with a line for Bojangles' that could inspire people to choose Bojangles' over Wendy's or McDonald's or Hardee's. While he was talking, Matt pressed play on a recorded stomach growl on his phone. A second later, a loud stomach growl was heard and it sounded like it was coming from Keith's belly. Keith grabbed his midsection and yelled, "It's Bo Time!" He yelled it again, "It's Bo Time!" He looked around the room and turned and sprinted out of the room.

Everyone on the BooneOakley team ran out after him yelling "It's Bo Time! It's Bo Time!" We ran outside and around the building down the street, right in front of the window of the basketball court, so that the Bojangles' clients would see us run by. We ran to the back door of BooneOakley, where we had a ton of Bojangles' food waiting. We each grabbed bags and boxes of food and tea. We turned and ran back around the building by the window to the basketball court and back into the front door. We returned to the basketball court with a lot of food, with our craving for Bojangles' satisfied.

"I've never seen anything like that before in my life," laughed Randy Kibler.

"Well, when you get a craving for Bojangles', you drop whatever you're doing and go get it," Keith said to him. "When 'It's Bo Time,' 'It's Bo Time.'"

"I really like it, and you know what I like about it?" Randy Poindexter said, "It reminds me of 'It's showtime' or 'It's go time.' It's time to do something."

Mike nodded in agreement.

"This is it. I think we have a new campaign," said Kelsey.

The Bojangles' team decided on the spot to go with "It's Bo Time!" There was no sending it through committee after committee to approve it. A focus group was never mentioned. They did something that very few marketers do these days. They listened to their gut. Which is a very good thing to listen to when you're selling chicken and biscuits.

*LISTEN TO YOUR GUT.

We had no idea how big "It's Bo Time" would become. We were just happy to have sold a campaign that we believed in.

Our strategic goal with the campaign was to help Bojangles' "own" craving. But something even bigger has happened. "It's Bo Time!" has helped Bojangles' own hunger. It's also helped them grow from 380 stores when "It's Bo Time!" was introduced in 2010 to over 600 as of December 2014.

I bet this guy spends a lot of time in the drive-thru.

AFTERWORD

THANKS FOR TAKING THE TIME TO READ MY STORIES. Living them was a blast. Writing them was even more fun.* But sharing them is the best. I certainly hope you enjoyed them.

Life is a series of stories. They happen every day. A friend recently told me that her mantra is "Wake Up And Live." Her hope every day is to wake up, get out, and live life. I now share her mantra. The only difference is that in the evening, I write about it.

---

*OK, honestly, writing them wasn't as fun as living them.

ACKNOWLEDGMENTS

I'D LIKE TO THANK EVERYONE AT BOONEOAKLEY FOR HELPING ME LOOK GOOD AND COVERING FOR ME WHILE I OBSESSED ABOUT WRITING THIS BOOK.

I was so thrilled when my mentor, Professor John Sweeney, agreed to write the foreword, and even more thrilled to read the cool things he said about me.

To:

My amazingly talented and wise editor, Betsy Thorpe, for getting me through this process and making it fun along the way.

My copyeditor, Maya Packard, for helping make the stories better and catching at least 200 typos.

My designer, Diana Wade, for laying out the book.

My wife Claire, for putting up with me for 25 years, but more importantly for being my best friend and soul mate.

My daughter Sydney, for her constant encouragement and always asking me, "Have you been writing, Dad?"

My son Lucas, for helping me understand how boring baseball really is and giving me so much material to write about.

My parents, Sid and Pat Oakley, who taught me to believe in myself and always encouraged me to do what I loved. They also instilled in me a "make-it-happen" attitude and the entrepreneurial spirit.

My sister Lisa, who is my biggest fan. I happen to be her biggest fan too. We are twins separated by three years.

My Aunt Hallie Oakley, whose story about Otis Collier is the funniest thing I've ever heard.

Pam and Joe D'Andrea, for being the best in-laws ever.

Randy Poindexter, Mike Bearss, Clifton Rutledge, Doug Poppen, Randy Kibler, and the entire Bojangles' organization for being such wonderful partners.

David Sedaris, for writing stories that inspired me to write.

Rene Hodges, for always encouraging me to write, calling me Shitbird, and always making me laugh.

Eric Roch von Rochsburg and Kara Noble, for designing the cover.

Luke Sullivan, whose book *Hey, Whipple, Squeeze This* totally reignited my passion for the advertising business.

Scott Corbett, for being a true friend and sounding board throughout this process.

Mike Carroll, for shooting a wonderful cover photograph for the book.

Peter Coughter, for being Dr. Coughter and teaching me so much about life and pitching.

Jim Mountjoy, for being a mentor, a friend, a confidant, and a damn good judge of wine.

David Baldwin, Susan Credle, Matt Porter, Jenn Snyder, and Tommy Tomlinson: thank you so much for reading the book and saying nice things about it.

Mike Hughes, for being the best boss I ever had.

My Vegas Boyz: Brad Oakley, Jim Doyle, Patrick Magner, Kurt Kitterman, Brian Knob, Jason Brannon, and GW Mix.

Caesars Palace and the Total Rewards Visa Card: thanks in advance for hooking me up next March.

Laura Wallace, Ashley Reker, Mary Gross, Emily Haney, Laura George, Dan Barron, Keith Greenstein, Kristin Kelly, Matt Klug, and Kathryn Bolles, for reading my stories and pretending to like them.

John Adams, Harry Jacobs, and Don Just, for teaching me The Martin Way.

Sam Frowine, for being a friend, a guide, and a coach.

Burnice Sparrow, for being a fantastic role model, for always being there for my family, and for being my dad's best friend.

Cynthia Zigmund, for helping me get this project started.

Jeff Alphin and Jane Brettschneider, for being Jeff and Jane.

Laura Bowen Kury, for drawing those pathetic stick figures at Chapel Hill.

Gale Bonnell, Mark Bartlett, and Adams Outdoor, for helping us bring so many great ideas to life.

Ted Williams, Trip Park, Taylor Busby, Tracy Tuten, Jayanta Jenkins, Charla Muller, Craig Chandler, and Greg Johnson, for encouraging me to write this book.

Jeremy Davids, for being a larger than life inspirational figure.

Bailey Hurt and Brad Tucker, for being my first mentors.

Susan King, for being the second best dean ever at Carolina (behind Dean Smith).

Nell Eaton, for teaching me to read and write.

John Boone, for being a great creative partner and for letting me put my name upside down.

If your name is not listed, it's not because I'm a complete moron. I didn't forget to put your name in here. I left it out on purpose. Simply because I know you like to avoid the spotlight. You are the most humble person I've ever met. I could never have done it without you. You helped me more than all the people that I've listed combined. You know who you are. That's right. It's you.

CPSIA information can be obtained at www.ICGtesting.com
Printed in the USA
BVOW10s0847030215

386081BV00009B/15/P